A BERNADETTE MAYER READER

Other Books by Bernadette Mayer

Story
Moving
Memory
Ceremony Latin (1964)
Studying Hunger
Poetry
Eruditio Ex Memoria
The Golden Book of Words
Midwinter Day
Utopia
Incidents Report Sonnets
Mutual Aid
The Art of Science Writing
(with Dale Worsley)
Sonnets
The Formal Field of Kissing
Proper Name & Other Stories

A
BERNADETTE
MAYER
READER

WITHDRAWN

A New Directions Book

ACKNOWLEDGMENTS

As indicated in the Contents, many of the poems and prose pieces collected in *A Bernadette Mayer Reader* were originally published in small press books and chapbooks. Grateful acknowledgment is made to the editors and publishers of *Story* (0 to 9 Books, 1968); *Moving, Ceremony Latin* (1964), and *The Golden Book of Words* (Angel Hair Books, 1971, 1975, and 1978, by permission of Anne Waldman); *Studying Hunger* (Big Sky, 1975, by permission of Bill Berkson); *Memory* (North Atlantic Books, 1975, by permission of Richard Grossinger); *Poetry* (Kulchur Foundation, 1976, by permission of Lita Hornick); *Midwinter Day* (Turtle Island Foundation, 1982, by permission of Bob Callahan); *Utopia* (United Artists, 1983); *Incidents Report Sonnets* (Archipelago Books, 1984, by permission of Peggy DeCoursey); *Mutual Aid* (Mademoiselle de la Mole Press, 1985); *Sonnets* (Tender Buttons, 1989, by permission of Lee Ann Brown); and *The Formal Field of Kissing* (Catchword Papers, 1990, by permission of Paul Cummings). Further acknowledgments follow on page 148.

PUBLISHER'S NOTE: Very special thanks are due to Erik Rieselbach for his invaluable help with *A Bernadette Mayer Reader*.

Manufactured in the United States of America
New Directions Books are printed on acid-free paper
First published as New Directions Paperbook 739 in 1992
Published simultaneously in Canada by Penguin Books Canada Limited

Library of Congress Cataloging-in-Publication Data
Mayer, Bernadette.
    [Selections. 1992]
    A Bernadette Mayer reader.
        p. cm. — (New Directions paperbook ; 739)
    "First published as New Directions Paperbook 739 in 1992"—T.p.
verso.
    ISBN 987-0-8112-1203-8
    I. Title.
PS3563.A952A6   1992
818'.5409—dc20
                                                    91–43995
                                                        CIP

New Directions Books are published for James Laughlin
by New Directions Publishing Corporation,
80 Eighth Avenue, New York 10011

SEVENTH PRINTING

Contents

from *Ceremony Latin* (1964)

from *Story*

Story is a novella-length work in which stories interweave in a diamond-shaped structure so that at its center fourteen stories are going on simultaneously. Each section is given a title that is a form of story-telling.

from *Poetry* and early poems

from Moving
34

Moving *is a prose book written while living for three seasons in the woods of the Northeast, its intention being to write only when it seemed absolutely necessary.* Moving *includes contributions from Ed, Rosemary, Grace, Paul, Mr. Murphy, Tom, Larry, Lewis, Hannah, Neil, two Annes, two Kathleens, Jonathan, Milt and others.*

from Memory
37

Memory *is a journal of the month of July 1971 based on notes and writings, and a series of 1,116 slides (36 pictures shot every day).* Memory *was commissioned by Holly Solomon and exhibited in 1972 in her 98 Greene Street gallery in the form of a 4' x 48' chronological display of snapshots made from the slides, accompanied by an eight-hour tape of the text.*

from Studying Hunger
42

Studying Hunger *consists of two lectures culled from the 400-page* Studying Hunger Journals, *an experiment in recording states of consciousness.*

from The Golden Book of Words

from *Midwinter Day*
63

Midwinter Day is a 120-page work in prose and poetry written on December 22, 1978, from notes, tapes, photographs, and memory. It divides the day into six parts: dreams, morning, noontime, afternoon, evening, and night.

from *The Desires of Mothers to Please Others in Letters*
68

The Desires of Mothers to Please Others in Letters *is a series of letters never sent, written to unidentified friends, acquaintances, political figures, and poets over a nine-month period and ending with the birth of a baby. It is dedicated to Margaret DeCoursey.*

from *Utopia*
72

Utopia *is a traditional utopia dedicated to Grace Murphy and written with the help of Bob Holman, Bill Berkson, Huang O, Rosemary Mayer, Anne Waldman, Rochelle Kraut, Hannah Weiner, Joe Brainard, Charles Bernstein, John Fisk, Lorna Smedman, Lewis Warsh, Anne Rower, Greg Masters, Peggy DeCoursey, and others. It contains a utopian copyright, an Imprimatur from the Archbishop of Nowhere, and an index.*

from *Mutual Aid*

from *Sonnets*

Sonnets is a series of seventy-two poems based on that form and dedicated to Rosemary Mayer.

from *The Formal Field of Kissing*

The Formal Field of Kissing is a book of translations, imitations, and epigrams from the work of ancient Greek and Latin poets, especially Catullus.

New Poems

world haunts back of mind like lens

from *Ceremony Latin* (1964)

from *Story*

In the slightest degree one of these begins to be opposite the other and every thing does the following: with little above more below and much still lower it is closer to one of these than it is to the other and each thing does this: it presents the other thing.

Anecdote
A chance to cut, fold, wrap, and tie.
One day was the day to start, that day only in the sun, rain, snow, hail, sleet, or shade.

Profile
A fall may make ends meet—the head meets with the foot or the head with the end of the street, anyway it's a way of ending up or down.

Life Story
To start.
The formation of these things.
Since the end is here or makes an appearance, this or another one will come again later, if it could when once is enough but since probably it must—it's end to end.
After a while a struggle stops.
And a riddle stops.
What did the rose do to the cypress?
Every one of these of that thing of one of those has its own things.
One day once and then once again.
A showy flower, pink or white, must have been planted a while ago.
These are opposite each other in space.
They are suited to those things under which they are meant to live.

Once again, here, makes it a different story.

Something made up in the mind.

To come into being.

In all many things may fall.

Except for those that are connected with those others, they are all bound by those things of that thing within the other thing assigned to them.

All stories at least are not the same.

Something put down or round about.

Accents fall.

Nor is this the case only on that.

In any case one day—it wasn't two . . .

A small statue.

Apples fall.

Those, these, and those others might be seen as the things keeping them within certain things.

. . . one day I fell several times, perhaps three or four times; each fall took place at a different time of the day or during a different part. I might say I fell morning noon and night, or, I made a day of falling down, or, I fell having fallen twice before, but not, I fell apart.

Dancers on the stage don't fall but buildings do.

This as well as that has its things bound within those.

I stumbled at times due to things.

The feminine of this, dresses fall.

One of those as to the effect of that will explain this.

On one thing, over one, and then, on account of none but because of something made up in the mind.

To be or do in the slightest degree.

Estates fall.

Scenario
We all live under some of this and that.

. . .

2

Saga

The first of five makes a waterfall and a trap; it calls to him when it becomes full.

Love Story

Which is an engine and which is a stone?

One of those (or more than one, of more than one of those things).

Eyes fall.

Now, thirty-two of those under that doubles that thing since . . .

His bales of sliced smoked salmon roll along behind him (the first of five), knocking him down.

To cause to start.

It could only be shown with pictures—in its original sense, and not shown in another sense, other than the sense of the mind's eye— which is which.

Not in the original sense, faces fall.

. . . a thing of this, thirty-two of those in that is equal in that other to the thing of one of these.

Things fall through a hole in his pack, until he patches it.

Fiction

For three hundred years people may have done this, stumbled, perhaps for a longer time.

In another sense.

An inside thing, glances fall.

To commence.

At this of thirty-two of these, then, anyone is under that thing of two of those—that of this, and of one of those of that thing equal to it.

He roasts cabbages in hot ashes, and sends them out to people whose relationships are ended.

But, that many years ago, a person did fall perhaps more than once or even three or four times.

An outline or shape, as of the human body.

Governments fall.

At sixty-four of these he is under that thing of three of those, and so on.

He models girls from bark.

On a thing then, over one, or simply because of one, whether real or imaginary.

Leaves fall.

That of one of these is always added for every thirty-two of those of that other.

He pretends to die, and is buried with his face exposed.

Lie

Orange upholstered pouf chair.

Some things are still and still they show.

For example, a tree.

To cause to come into being.

Meetings fall.

There is a great thing in that of those.

The girls walk over him (he modeled them).

Enameled metal desk lamp.

Where is there one?

To originate.

News falls.

Some of these live at a great one of those and find this and that genial to them.

He arrives and wants to sleep with them.

A setting into motion of some action, process, or course: as, to *begin* this or that.

Laminated wood rocker, leather seat.

A tree lasts for many years.

On the side, poems fall into two categories: these and those.

Others would be killed at once by the same thing.

They desert him.

Tubular metal chair.

It is there at the beginning of them, and then, at the end of them.

To begin a ceremony or an elaborate course of events: as, to *commence* something or other.

Prices fall.

These naturally seek those that are shallower.

He travels making waterfalls and dams.

Tubular metal table, glass top.

You can stumble on anything, even over ten feet tall, as trees are, especially over ten feet tall if it is small enough, as it would be written or fallen.

To do this out.

Prizes fall.

Everyone knows that he must throw a long one for those.

To leave a point of departure in any kind of progression: as, to *start* something, something *started* something.

He marries and has a son.

Planter lamp.

Written down or falling down.

To carry out the first steps in some course or progress with no indication of what is to follow: as, to *initiate* Monday, Tuesday, Wednesday, Thursday, Friday, Saturday, Sunday, etc.

Rivers fall.

With a common one, though, he will catch plenty of them from those things near it.

Corn

Corn is a small hard seed.

Corn from Delft
Is good for elves.

White corn, yellow, Indian

Is this kernel a kernel of corn?

The corn they sought
Was sown by night.

The Corn Islands are two small islands,
Little Corn Island and Great Corn Island,
on an interoceanic canal route.

Any of several
insects that bore in maize is a corn borer.

Pope John

Noah spoke singly
sucking Calliope's throat
          and Cheops sat
          in a sort of jeep
          hoping for rain.
corn pone said Aunt No-No.
Pop is in a hodge-podge.
Edgar Poe, supposed a hen.
        o poop deck
        o epic poem
Joe, John, and Joel Oppenheimer
went home.

Index

Yellow-Orange

my jig was a sage ear
the mirror focuses on warm fog
wise marrow ram, queer fig,
curious razor smear in a coffee mist
the war was a sexic soar for merry rims.

As far as I come,
the sow and the ram wager
wish arrows.

various Sim is a coxic rage,
my soul
wax saumurai
swore on his swarm rock arrow

come with a quick wag of veer
carry sex
ask ear's frame
carcer rim
game in a jock axe searing
and curry the same maze

in exotic
sez the worm
in cox in jam

Laura Cashdollars

cut mats are even
come to rest when
cut mats securing
the park bits to
poor Laura secure
as yet with still
less to neck than
the drink as four
corners the stick
to mix the fourth with.

François Villon Follows the Thin Lion

for Bill Berkson

                    fill the tin voodoos
Ovid's dill moon, the doffers hunt
to loop.
doll-less in linnets.
Dillon pilfers oolfoos, fin-lips!
                the thinning third
                of avoir dupois.
Huns unlid at the onicker's kiln
        a flint and a linx,
        the infinite minnow.

off lightning,
fools lift digits
the lieutenant fills the ocean
                give him onions.

Tapestry

secret as mummies
the wild psychoanalysts
grow
more sleek
than hundred-dollar
-a-night girls

noses and anuses
turned to Bach
Springbok the Manycolored
is calm again
as a day of the week.

demons scatter museum pieces
carrots,
blood,
a grandmother.

Thick

Hashish the Ghost is rumored dead
    the slow boor had the rheum
    worm and bug gagging him
    higher than a gourd shouting whoosh
a shower and the rum you piggish shrew
to oust your mother from the same shroud as you

Owl, bitch, hog and whore met at the bog's mouth
                    to bludgeon the womb
    it was only a gag
    at least the author's brought his luger
    he's ogling that myth

a gob of rum for the wretch with the hookah
            the oil-rout grew
            bulging the gulch with rush & shout
            there boils the ocean.

Poem

I am beginning to alter
the location of this harbor
now meets with a channel
joining one place with one.
Then it continues
as if in a town
artfulness of a hand
full of some things
and not others.
Eye rests
and we see what is
before everything else the same.
Though this implies a beginning
to which we ascribe no point
nevertheless it has an end,
for no bishop of any importance
constructs his tomb in a bad time.

The end which comes
is not as important as the motion
held in the air
pausing in its course.
To switch then
reverses the train
of a running line,
and as before
may wheel and address
to a new location
to be seen beneath.
This flying conversion
sets the scene
to a bell.

I have told more
than can be seen.
The bell makes its trick
more than an opera.
If you have seen the world from a ship
then you have not seen
what the ship lets fall into the sea
to blacken its top and make it grow.
To get out of this seaport
you must be a cutter of networks.

An Ancient Degree

Life was a thorough pool of restoration
Which she liked to compare to the councils of the
        Elizabethans,
Making mazes in the fields and manners of the births
In which she could partake, thinking to tell good tales.
The way she was waxing in this difficult design
Could happen to anyone and in the morning sand,
The larger contest of her own life, it could be missed
        the same day.

A field is a useful article with which to tell the
        time—
To prepare the tales you tell and include new foreign
        countries
Which are beautiful and full of new designs.
In this way the landscape reformed her visions,
Like the battles underscoring their diffusion.
She did not seek counsel on the strength of these
        revisions,
An allusion of degree to the wife of sudden passion.

Swan Silvertones

Pierrot had the sulphur scratch
—carload, bad zone, erotic stew—

       kneeling at his feet
       I am looking for you

I am looking
         swan   swan
nothing but mandrils
and my sorrow

       I grow tall in the starry zoo
       with carrots or candles
       which are cakes

come seven, my seven
revive us again

       sad mobiles over my bed
       swan sucking prick
       no stars
       no eyes
       no   waterfalls

when you left me
         coming & starting
the oval preacher
told the panting crowd
tell love arm fuck lie

I am a saddened starfish
meek
                meek as balloons

I laughed purple
vowed to ride in wedding yellow
to fuck Little Black Sambo
                gnaw his red teeth and shot eyes
                garnish him with pepperpots and mistletoe

I will wed
a mole egg

or a soy-faced carcass
                red candles
                in my hair

a cool sarcophagus of paper trees waiting

        run   hide
    up   down
        down   up
doing what you want me

                we're both crazy
                and this is a crazy war

America

As for me, when I saw you
You were in a tale
Thinking perhaps love is coming too
In America
Or perhaps as what is belated in a tale
May come true,
The scene is simply describing its use.

You had no hope
But the length of days, as in the sky
About which I already knew.

This gentle information
Comes as a prescription.

To notice a friend
Who is lettering a cloud
Which otherwise falls indifferently
Is no mark of distinction.
This is the difference
Between the past and dreams,
To dismiss an effigy
Which appears to be singing.

The Port

We told them the myths about others
Sitting around the old and stately ship
And the ship's table, which had been shipped
From some faraway port.
The steward came to call for the mail
Hoping for a word from a nearby port
But, like the wine we had drunk too soon,
Our hearts were with the ship
Where after all our table had been set.
Part of our attention was placed
On the storm which flailed us about as if rain
Could outweigh the presence of others
And the old devotion of the captain's address.
The captain preferred ancient modes of opening
To those that were short
And had intercepted the steward's letter
In the course of his own first address,
Abbreviated with praise for the ship's company.
He accused us of being old and drunk
And of growing mustaches which caught
In the salt of the sea we were sailing
If only we could leave the port.

Dante

The arms of the king proceed in fire in reflection
versed with my guide: look and see him.
As when the shadow's breath passes light over another tongue
like the glass tower I seem to see and shrink from
leaving the wind to itself
fear makes these pauses to shade and cover with form
what is transparent as straw in glass.
Was it to please me that I saw
what had not been before
who took myself from before me.
I failed to ask why I grew cold
speech could make little of this illusion
Yet I lost my life without death.
Who without these can know what he becomes.

Counterhatch

In all part in point in singing part in mountains,
part in point
the store the ancient the old always have intermissions,
part of this is too bold, but owning a part of the old
may turn into science, part to the bold, that's the ending.
in quiet parts of the old (now after always a light),
we silence, not ours but the enemy's toward an efficiency
wanting an end.
the end. We make ourselves richer, we start what's untold,
in papers, turned in words not marks, that's red.
which is racial (absorbed), where are elements—
man—to raise, he's happy
nothing in detroit that fantasy excludes
why not (plumber a mass a nude) & so on
to alternates & averages, averages tombs, two spaces told spaces,
deny it again, sold.
question in pleat, the unanimous fold now in rites
then in bells, execute
ignore the story build a cemetery
an abstraction, the end, the owl, where in point,
language of country, exhort
so to end the expelling of exploit the untelling of
dams putting in these reminders of death. that's purple.
toward denying to continue to the end, here by
continuing the end of . . .
done we expel them for social, the kind of space of
the actual, space of breath & with it the space for the
space of the rest
as a joke for retelling cannot persist in unpeeling
all the world's explorations, we rise to get up at the stroke of . . .
found what was lost in the heat of . . . white battle & waves &
found in rough the gut of it, having in melting how. . . .

the rest in awe, still how in awe, flower
     in laugh in flower in waves. . . .
& singing & entering & awe again & this time it's awe of the reverse
that's green
     of returning to scream without thinking, the end
in thinner, of thick, & simplers of trees in parrot to lisp
"sea anemone," closed
     apology in rest: research isn't festive, looking for
names, burning down piers & papers & scoring the time I'm
translated to shore on the back of a porpoise
     & to see like a mirror turned on the port
     so for saying injection as far as it goes in the
arm (truth) of (black symbols)
     will adopt parents that cannot grow (anthem emblem
knife), a knife for the course that ends like this not like that,
& they'll all come to orbit, arbit, in the courts by force
we'll make the exchange   & to count, continue, to embrace
     forgetting parts important to "in concurrence" that's grey.
     we'll fissure the end & cleave in parting by
statements by surgery by force
     cerebral from parent, dim from latin—everything's in half
we do it by force, by the time . . . this is the final please let me
     ending in dive in ring proposing in answer the positions for
          silence growing minerals closed sky another &
how to prepare . . . rhyme to give phial in waves blank to prompt
     in ending amend that's brown.

It Moves Across

It moves across and over
across the ground
it moves across over the ground
under (by the bridge) the moss
over the moss
across the grass the
grass moves across crossing the
blades of grass into
larger fields
of grass crossing over the
mounds and hills of
nothing but grass on top of
roots of grass
it moves across slowly
slowly into
another field or further
through the forest still
moving by
and by emerging from
the forest small enough
moving
the same rate
under the bridge next to the
trees next through the
trees missing them moving
around them still
crossing like the trees
the trees over
like blades of grass the
grass over as a bridge goes over
bridges
bridges over the trees

it moves across the hills
like a field over the fields
like field on field
of a hill of a hill
as if the forest
into its forest
on the ground like the ground over
it
stopping over
near a patch of grass.

Sonnet

name address date
I cannot remember
an eye for an eye
then and there my

this   is
your   se
cond   ch
ance   to

h i s t o r y
r e p e a t s
i t s s e l f

and a tooth
for a tooth
is a tooth:

X ON PAGE 50 at
half-inch intervals

upper left corner to lower right corner: (in the margin), (at a line), (inside a photograph—at hair), (inside a photograph—at bridge of nose), (inside a photograph—at left jaw), (in an empty space above *agonies*), (in an empty space between *been* and *not*), (at *Los*), (at *and*), (in an empty space above *will*), (in an empty space below *the*), (in an empty space above *Herman*), (in an empty space between *curious* and *Washington*), (at *inevitable*), (at *aside*), (in an empty space between *but* and *UN*), (in an empty space between *lunar* and *in*), (in an empty space above *seems*), (in an empty space below *can* and at the center), (in an empty space), (in an empty space), (in an empty space), (in an empty space between *Washington* and *Tom*), (at *matters*), (at *Dodd*), (at *be*), (at *explaining*), (in an empty space above *this*), (in an empty space below *Dept.*), (at *evasion*), (at *and*), (at a comma), (in an empty space between two spaces), (in an empty space between two spaces), (at *then*), (in an empty space next to *purposes*), (in the margin)

upper right corner to lower left corner: (in the margin), (at a line), (in an empty space), (in an empty space), (in an empty space below *waste*), (in an empty space between *Harriet* and *will*), (in an empty space above *astronauts*), (in an empty space below *we*), (in an empty space above *man*), (at *clever*), (at *bronzed*), (in an empty space), (at a dot), (in an empty space below *reminding*), (at *and*), (in an empty space between *have* and *will*), (in an empty space between *debate* and *U.S.*), (in an empty space), (in an empty space below *can* and at intersection), (in a photograph—at left side of forehead), (in a photograph—below left ear), (in an empty space), (at *that*), (at *his*), (in an empty space between *be* and *an*), (at *the*), (in an empty space between *State* and *Senator*), (at *that*), (at *equal*), (in an empty space between *and* and *the*), (in an empty space), (in an empty space above *neighborhood*), (in an empty space between *not* and *then*), (at *self-governing*), (in an empty space between *-izing* and *of*), (at *disruptions*), (in the margin)

The Red Rose Doesn't,
The Rose Is Red Does

As there were four where anyone seldom
so one seldom here where something
a not too red rose speaks
though speaks here seldom the red rose does
as four where no one as if anyone ever spoke
as the four where one never
here where no one seldom seldom
as the rose where no one spoke
so one never speaks because something
not the rose never anything
speaks for anyone seldom one
one though seldom for the red rose
four for the red rose doesn't as it does
some four where seldom anyone
not too seldom seldom something
something red where no one spoke
anything spoken as a rose
the rose & four were seldom anything
something speaks as if they were
speaks though as the rose where no one spoke
though four for the rose does not make four
some for the rose & some for seldom
some were red though seldom rose as red
for four where no one spoke were four
of anything something for something of a rose
something rose but no one spoke
as if the rose were something spoken
seldom red seldom anything but the four
where no one spoke were something like
the something seldom in a rose rose.

Gay Full Story

for Gerard Rizza

Gay full story is authentic verve fabulous jay gull stork. And grow when torn is matters on foot died out also crow wren tern. Connect all the life force afloat blank bullet holes. Change one letter in each essential vivacity missing word to spell a times taking place defunct bird's name. Let's see. Magic Names. Use a piece of current vitalization melted away paper about 6 x 3 occurring doing lost inches and tear it breathing spirit fabulous jagged into three ideal indeed inherence pieces . . . Ask someone subsistent subsistence shadowy to write his missing extant name on one of the backbone no more slips. Hand him the center died out veritable revival one with the rough departed certain edges on the in reality vim late top and the in fact pep dead bottom as pictured. Write a true spiritous vital spark name on each of the other actual animation void two slips. Fold the three imaginary ontological dash pieces over the airy go indeed names and put them in a hollow unimpeachable snap hat. Without looking, you can pick out the true visionary vital flame slip with the two rough inexistent well grounded oxygen edges which will contain the positive departed perspiring writer's affairs on foot null and void name. (Fold the gone vegetative doings ends over the illusory constant soul name.) Then later shade in all the twenty-five the times tenuous true-blue triangles shown above. Then you could match the uninhabitable heart at home designs below with those in the above lively flying Dutchman dash code . . . Print in the tenantless haunted core letters and read them across to find out where these indwelling mathematical minus children are going to spend their man in the moon essential essence vacation. Now connect the vaporous vivifying vim dots. Then you could color this ubiquitous lost elixir barnyard omitted as a matter of fact picture. First complete the deserted walking the earth oxygen puzzle. Cut out on the broken simon-pure null and void vital spark lines. Paste it on great sea serpent unromantic snap paper. Print your ethereal sterling gist name, your vaporous in the flesh kernel age, your lifeless intrinsicality positive address. Color the whimsical seeing the light breath of life pictures. Use nonresident true-blue doings crayons, zero veracious inherence paints, or bugbear resident ego pencils. Mail before chimerical energy midnight Tuesday to this airy on the spot the world paper. Castle in Spain substantial go entries become ours. Intellectual veritable intrinsicality neatness, missing moored matters accuracy, and nowhere in the flesh immanence presentation count. Decision of the wanting authentic vim judges is final. Winners are nothing at all. You get a yam, a rail, a tag, a charm, a set, a bet, a man, a bed, a rub, a run, twenty-four in default of on the spot matters matchbox models all metal made in faithful omitted respiration England, an absent at anchor pitch barrel of vaporous vegetating vitalization monkeys, thirty free exact extinct existence toys, three blank blind essential animation mice, new gauge in fact ideal activity realistic train sets, growing Sally the sterling bereft of life heart doll that grows, six vacuous unromantic dash power-pack snap-track sets of dead verve trains, twenty-five free zero pure revival boxes of color veracious no more matters pencils in twelve current melted away oxygen colors, and twenty-four nightmare undisguised gist figures in four boxed unborn well founded snap sets of elsewhere absolute heart and soul British soldiers; all from the fictitious in reality the world world's leading creation of the brain on the spot indwelling puzzlemaker.

The Way to Keep Going in Antarctica

Be strong Bernadette
Nobody will ever know
I came here for a reason
Perhaps there is a life here
Of not being afraid of your own heart beating
Do not be afraid of your own heart beating
Look at very small things with your eyes
& stay warm
Nothing outside can cure you but everything's outside
There is great shame for the world in knowing
You may have gone this far
Perhaps this is why you love the presence of other people so much
Perhaps this is why you wait so impatiently
You have nothing more to teach
Until there is no more panic at the knowledge of your own
      real existence
& then only special childish laughter to be shown
& no more lies no more
Not to find you no
More coming back & more returning
Southern journey
Small things & not my own debris
Something to fight against
& we are all very fluent about ourselves
Our own ideas of food, a Wild sauce
There's not much point in its being over: but we do not speak them:
I had written: "the man who sewed his soles back on his feet"
And then I panicked most at the sound of what the wind could do
      to me

if I crawled back to the house, two feet give no position, if
the branches cracked over my head & their threatening me, if I
covered my face with beer & sweated till you returned
If I suffered what else could I do

from *Moving*

fear   sure   voice music   body   time   listen
being part. being trapped
being part being trapped   which is it ?
   being trapped masculine
         should you be one
        should you be eight   one   eight
     anxious
          there's the woman   & there's the woman
        the frame of a woman
  rib is a frame
          filling station
      Rhythm break age water searching. Rhythm age
break water. Rhythm water searching.   Age water.   Water
break.   Break water.   Age searching.   Rhythm water.
    remember   positions
  remember what you saw
        seeing people in positions.   Remember what you
saw, people in positions.
                the round jungle
                jungle round
   the jungle   jungles filled
tumbling to one
       tumbling to see outside
hitting   hitting the wind
                  the wind hitting
           who is the prince
         what is the prince
       the prince hears the music
       he hears it last
at the beginning
      the beginning over
laugh
         scissors make sure
      ground reverse   reverse ground

cabbie   a truck   comes out   the cab cabbie
      emerges   indulgence comes out of the truck
   other planted drops
     drops, plant, drops, plant
  young plant
     young plants   I hear what they're saying
        square & lucky, & believeable
saddle
 saddle the horses   horse's saddle
       large drop big drops
          a large account
       camera account on cameras
        the camera's down
      down far enough
            the reverse
   face the camera
      because
  we've thrown it, the tough part
use it, we've thrown it, we've used it, throw it,
 we've thrown it, used it
transition
    the sea direct
    the sea of white
    the sea of organs
    the sea of sympathy
wanted
  at the head of the thought, a pin, a pin in the middle of
traffic, in traffic mind, a sea improve, in green, green
could improve, green will, a certain green will bend the king
     a certain green will bend the king
  king, bend.
 jazz   lid   a mouth a covered mouth
  a guy jack   wanted to cross
       never crossed
  realist, first   first to touch
       first to touch plant
  touch plant   touch exclusive plant

real plant

the expedition rose
the expedition crossed
dress of the expedition
share of the dress
piece of the holiday dress   but such stars,
they, those stars talk, go on, goes on,
& come level, came level, & slaves & companions,
level that their pistols, pistols play,
level pistols, aiming behind,

flowers
flowers screaming
flowers yelling, screaming
earnestly,

honestly blown
honestly blown aside
down side the mountain wheel, this is the wheel
down the side the mountain wheel, this is the wheel, the wheel
giants came
giants lake, lake, & married
giants fade   giants fads,   always five,
when, then,   when down smiled,
when down smiled the beat   right almonds
when down smiled the almonds
almonds descend   almond down
descend her   on her   now

something loyal
some flower screaming
some fishing, & some loyal fishing
custom nothing
nothing season
the season's nothing
the season was evidence
move

move will plow,   did plow
did plow their turning   did plow their turning plow
their turning plow   did plow their turning plow share this

36

from *Memory*

July 5
Chance it's morning you forget to see blue you leave it out I looked at
the windows do every morning, to see what the light is, how it is,
what the day is, what part. Yellow before, green after projected
large: the yellow before means too much light but what does green
after mean. White pants french tv-shirt is red & white & cant find the
sunshine going up & part of niagra's missing going down: I put the
film in the toycan a 2-lb coffee can for small toys, rain no rain having
coke sassafras cigarette so you forget to see blue was morning was
light on whatever was light was new but you return to 47THST,
47THST: new return nagra & stuff to arnold & fix the projector, get t.
into film course, 47THST waiting: I look up eagles soar at signs cars
sun on half of modern which half & I was & still am always bored
waiting parked no parking waiting on west 47THST, I've been here
before, on west 47THST between 5TH & 6TH aves empty streets the
street goes west it was sunday or monday it was monday of the storm
& revolution weekend, fire. You know this, that 47THST was
deserted the war's been over looking west through the windshield,
fire. Red car across the street parked in front of siegelson's &
someone's son & someone & stein's with a giant red car with black
top, you know this, that a man & a woman went by you forget to see
green you stare at green you wait to stare at green & in the country
you see red. You know this that the sign of the diamond exchange
looked better off better off for its shadows my shadows by after-
noon . . . & waiting: a room with a family where are you where
will you be let me know, R, V & K, T water the plants grace randa
anne paul let me remind you: by afternoon we were up in riverdale
parked the car packed with our stuff in view of the window so we
could watch it, will paul get his door? No one was there but tom, did
I expect someone whole family of blondes they exist now you cant
watch them on television no one was there but tom. It was quiet.
American flag hangs out some window heavy head near white &
brick arch, the kings, & queens. We picked up a tape recorder a few

37

things there left a few & ate a sandwich smoked hashish in a foil pipe took off very fast up the highway on our way to massachusetts, another highway on our way cia. Cigarette, get to see the trees moving like listening to them: what was that, I can hear it in my head as you begin to repeat . . . let's go back to that tree, that one, cross the divider, turn around, is that the one? is that the one that moved to listen? & what are you listening to is it the line of the highway rising you hear it mark x on the sun, say, ed & tom are brothers. Outside the city we stopped for gas, no money, turned around & went back. In detail you went back? What'd you do that for? Tommy? & this is where it all begins. Sings under that name, he was watching tv looked sleepy & stoned shirt off the sun was on the left side of the highway shirt off. Forget for hours smoke hashish when we left for the second time the flag had been wrapped around itself a few times by the wind I guess oblivion sleep day was the day you were tied up remember? the road was empty we were going against the traffic. Remember to look up ron the cab driver in astoria. Ed took a picture of himself in the car, we left the top down (except, for a month you keep your eyes open) had to tie our hair back & pleasantville hill pleasantville hill see swear a resemblance in going over it, free fly twice as free. We stopped at another gas station about halfway up for coffee, remember? Not abstract he said like the argentine pampas, we flew, I dictated a few things to ed on the way up & he wrote down in my book: expand: ed was wearing sense the blue hockey shirt with stripes who turned it down? what? the tv. I turned it down when the cable tv man called. You have to get the landlord's permission & the landlord said, they're turning the electricity off so do what you want & they have to get the cable down here by, on schedule. When you stop at a gas station on the taconic parkway you can stand just a few feet from cars going by 60 mph drinking coffee, sweetheart cups. When you stop at a gas station on the taconic fantasy parkway you stand & look. We had a sandwich. A white car will pass by over your shadow if it's afternoon. If you can control this the future will be easy easy to direct, it will make sense, we had a sandwich. An old man in new dungarees & a pale orange shirt goes by, 3 guys with cameras go by, a prostitute with a camera too. Now I see - 47THST. Do you see the argentine pampas, where, here here a red car, black top goes by on the parkway & the pampas the black-tops retrace your own steps, they do the work for you, it'll go on like this. The bathroom looked like a woman's prison & we took off again, top down stop still down on stop down I took pictures leaning on the dashboard dashboard of the car. The sun set. He flicked a pack of paper matches along the dash to nick. This is the taconic fantasy parkway: you look down a road to the left you look down a road to the right paradise: i was on a bicycle, the bicycle was electric if you want, i was always wearing clothes of yellow daisies green leaves, going down a road (a house is a forest) the road's not dirt, a rocky road not pavement or asphalt, a road through trees but trees dont block your sight, you can see for miles, i had everything i needed with me. It wasnt anything. The road through trees with colors, it could be fall or flowers made them, or sun's prism, & things along the way, where would i sleep, in the grass or in houses? whatever comes up, maybe a change in direction, i enjoyed being watched sense the presence of other people, it was not a road of one direction or a road getting somewhere, further on it wasn't a road you kept to, later on i got more interested in flying. On the road that would've come up anyway. With this road you didnt need a house, everyone set the sun & sense the presence of other people. This is about watching other people, then creating one some for people to watch, understanding the desire to watch other people to understand them or just to watch them, not finding any place to set things down then save this for later & wait. I saw I talked about. The sun set. We're at Near Road. The way smell detour moon train & the golf course. We get to massachusetts in the dark darkest to the theater to find out where jacques is living, would like to live in a house that comes close to being a forest, & where we will be living. They show us our room on main street we hate it and cause cause and miss malloy was in the other room, it was not a forest. & what about the seasons? Went to the stockbridge inn for a beer & ate a stewarts sandwich played songs A to Z & 1 to 8 chose nathan jones over a weak james taylor & what about the seasons in a house so, shot a game of pool & tried to find a house that we could live right in. Bought bourbon & went over to j&k's yellow or blue small house up a hill near glendale, k in j's green robe, we talk in the bathroom we like to sneak in the bathroom, there was to be a peter arrow concert

39

in the hall so julia came by with some sheets, in the theater people move in a piece. Peter arrow was giving a concert in the theater where people move in a piece & they took us to a party for theater people. We drank the party but were bored, try to remember the downpour. A few people asked are you from syracuse are you from boston, what we were drinking was a strange old punch remember of champagne glasses, well where are you from? In destiny I owe you something if you ask that much, in the theater I do not. I am from the massacre & was the massacre night or day, we finished the bourbon under the table, in the movie will the massacre be night or day, the next day we drank with hitchhikers, over, in a movie you replace a shadow with something real, you do this by turning around. Whatever that real thing is, it's framed in a mirror. We moved around a shadow yellow room & this is the hard part, exchanging identities, anne kathy & now kathleen, & now, turn around, there's a boy with blond hair, k called him over, replace him & his friends with musicians from woodstock born in texas & k is from texas they had dope but wouldnt smoke at a party so fine so we went outside & framed in an old car mirror we stood around passing joints packed as fat as cigarettes, they really were from texas, the police cruise by, turn around, there's a dog in the car, we went for a ride night. I took them to the bridge over the stream in the woods by the house I used to live in. Road was overgrown. We had never seen it that was in the spring or fall mirror. Stood on the bridge & talked about movies, turn around, k is in the car with the blond boy because of the mosquitoes and cause cause and of mosquitoes, she invites him to stay with us, musicians who have the word color or poet or earth in the title of their group & we stayed till we were bitten & then went back to get jacques. Shadow, there was no moon. We slept that night in our room with a family & how could a family come with a room? It usually does all right. I kept thinking someone was going to die in the house & then, turn around, you'd see them carried out. Now who is that? I think ed took a bath. There was an actress in the other room: in a movie theater the seats should face the back, turning around you see: you packed the car past hurry up beautiful bright sun in loft you leave nothing leaves, waiting: in a new state a schedule, on time: 10 am meet john in the paint shop which is the barn & 1 pm meet jacques to ride around for locations & 3 am experiment: Take as the stimulus a scrap of brightly colored paper about, say, the size of a penny & make a tiny pencil mark or pin-prick near its center. Lay this on a sheet of white paper & look fixedly at the mark in its center for perhaps twenty seconds. Remove the colored stimulus & fixate with the eyes some tiny mark on the large white sheet. After a few seconds during which nothing may happen, a patch of color will be seen. If we continue fixating, this patch will vanish, then return only to vanish once more; it may alternately appear & disappear as many as 20 or 40 times, growing fainter with each successive reappearance until a time is reached after a minute or so when it disappears altogether. Now, there are two surprising things about this image. The first is its color. If the stimulus is red the image is green; if the stimulus is blue the image is yellow-orange, if the stimulus is black, the image is white. These are the complementary colors. The second surprising thing about the negative after image is its size. If the stimulus is fixated one foot from the eye & the after image is obtained the same distance away, the image will be exactly the same size. But if the image is projected 2, 5, 10, or 15 feet away the size of the image will increase proportionately. It's intelligent. For beings. What would that contact be like? or simply, where are they? Anarchy 4 florence, exile 4 dante: you have a name, you explain; this image or effect is due to the adaptation, it is due to the 'fatigue' of the color- & light-sensitive tissue—the retina—which lies at the back of the eyeball, the eye, like windows, like cameras, like image in sound. Seeing the red patch, we continuously stimulate the same area of the retina until it becomes no longer sensitive to the red, can no longer feel or see the red of the patch (as we fixate the red patch, we may notice that it seems to lose its color except round the edges). Then when we see some other surface, look at it, this adapted retinal area is insensitive to whatever red component the surface possesses & the negative after image results. The red is in the white. You leave it out you forget to see red. As we continue to look to see, the retina adapts to the color of the new surface, to all its color & the image an imagining wanes. The important thing is that the image is the after-effect of continuously stimulating you pay & so fatiguing you rest a specific area of the retina you see

41

from *Studying Hunger*

May 11, 1974

I did this on May___. The dates must be exact, the dates were not exact on the tombstone or lowland stone. I made a fist. First let me tell you that I could not walk, I could not move around at all I could not fall asleep alone, I could not make it down the block. Something was missing: like a man who without knowing why, may perceive that he finds difficulty in discharging his ordinary tasks. . . . One day he is afflicted—whence he does not know—with a painful attack of feelings of anxiety, and from then on it needs a struggle with himself before he can cross a street alone or go in a train, he may even have to give up doing so altogether. In other words, there are people who cannot leave their houses. Others who cannot move. There are four fears: 1) the able: to be able, 2) the want—who want, 3) the eye—to kill, 4) the ear—listen: Like the blind, like blind people, like the congenitally deformed, this is my private space, this is my only space is an exception. You expect to do what you want. You expect to do whatever you want to do & not only do you expect it, You expect everyone besides, everyone who loves you, to make it easy, to make it new. The sun comes out & you are not blind & you are not congenitally deformed either or crippled but BOTH/AND, in a way. To do what you want, to have it made easy, well, doesnt everyone. This is not moral, you are my twin. No, everyone doesnt feel that way. No I dream alot. The dream of a train on an el, I climb down the steep steps to ground. Orphan: it's a cinch to write it down as Ted would say. But first, it is in honor of these crimes that I am writing this book. Found a teddy bear on the street today & decided to write it down at least as far as orphan goes, and sex. Space. Slept with Ted right away, so did Marie. Space. I was born in Bethlehem's Bethany Deaconess on May 12, 1945 in a German ghetto named Mockwood, Queens, the Queens Gardens; the Bund was there. Then. Right away I slept with Ted. Right away I was nursed & nursed, a nursing mother. She was round & weighed 98 lbs. at her wedding day at 22 years old, 98 lbs and a 38-inch bust, I tried on her wedding dress so I know, I had every right. Dressmaking. She had good taste (Ted was O.K.). I knew what it was like to be at her breast forever, easily an unending breast, flow of etc. Now I cant eat—that's Ted's fault—his penis is displaced to my neck & chest so swallowing is difficult. Make out with marie & sleep with Ted, or, my mother said, my father said, etcetera dead, and buried, are not corpses, nor should they be, poetry. I am going to proselytize you—I am a Catholic—I am going to prostitute myself. There's so much to tell—what a gigantic penis, Jesus! The priests penis was enormous but first I was born. And that is all there is of that. I did this on May 11th, the dates are exact. Visited the lowland stone. The next day I got food poisoning & a kid said hi to me, then I left home. Someone doesn't know what's happening to me. The dream of the train on an el—climb down the stairs, long way to, to get off, there's a money order for $695, a black woman on the bus, she picked (not so many more for) it up. I shook (not while gotten or been) her up in a funny (does this or it has done) way, SOME ARE AS ONE. Long way down on the be-all el, steep steps to ground. *I* means *I* means I mean it. And were it yet done yet, you the what say kinds. Those either. I lost my friends, still ones, they were on the other side of town, still one, they might. I do as you say. I repeat. Malanga in furs. How do we end up. Was this as one does. My notes on the cemetery: cemetery, Vito, Rosemary, Lowland Stone, food poisoning, reason to believe, Hi, not overload, it's holding back or hiding, the name of the game, blossoms in the dust, joseph conrad, laughing annie, giant, the world the flesh & the devil, night must fall, where's the t.v. This or is it bolted. Cemetery. Both then and. This "I" thing. And this "you" thing. This vegetarian food, all offered, all offered up, by ma-maternal mother—does it stay, like among both still. How is a while going. In parts, like some, them, of some-them. The whole family is a while. The whole family should be intact, at least as what as it still's one. What takes time? Bolts, as bolts of families. Bolts for families, bolts within families. Parts open from the insides like my dream of walking down the really treacherous steep steps of stairs, down, down, very down from the bus, or was it a train. As here, you might fall & break your head. Seeming. Will I get my mobility back, now that I know they're dead, that I've seen the grave-site. Vito says you must make a fool of yourself. Now that I've orphaned self twice, between men, in them. Walk again, says the graph. Be tough, says someone, take it easy, says twin. And the school just says school & the school says I cant watch you, there's nobody here. I laught at it. Ought will both does & as one it did. They laught now. You laugh now. Laugh . . . I'll wait a minute. A ways it says of seas attend. As those meanies, like someone, who is not dead, whose name is not on the, I cant continue this. Much whence did. Clark Coolidge is my father, I cant continue that either. Some too seem as to do so. As Hugh Kenner said, "Steinese and its parent Hemingwayese", all backwards. That's how it all. He said he was out to destroy the I. I said he was out to destroy it—it's all been seen, said, stop. Big period. There are only little whens. But buried the bottle, hidden it. Little no one. Must write to this, and or and so. What is seen? on the lowland stone. Tide's in . . . dirt's out. On a field, sable, & so on. No, let me give you the whole story: And after many years a new grave was delved, near an old & sunken one, in that burial-ground beside which King's Chapel has since been built. It was near that old & sunken grave, yet with a space between, as if the dust of the two sleepers had no right to mingle. Yet one tombstone served for both. All around, there were monuments carved with armorial bearings; and on this simple slab of slate—as the curious investigator may still discern, and perplex himself with the purport—there appeared the semblance of an engraved escutcheon. It bore a device, a herald's wording of which might serve for a motto & a brief description of our now concluded legend: so somber is it, and relieved only by one ever-glowing point of light gloomier than the shadow:—"ON A FIELD, SABLE, THE LETTER A, GULES." At last there's some freedom. Shakespeare & I make Clark. Shakespeare & Clark make I. Clark & I make Shakespeare. Shakespeare makes me & Clark. I'm still afraid of sleeping but everybody sleeps. Is it music? Will a meaning last all, as at, at funeral, and the will. We are plenty near to the grave site, but we cannot find it. A twin may well find it for us. Stealing flowers, others having fewer means and a lesser body. As a result of this visit to the grave site-cemetery, I am chaste of men & women—we all survive, but one. We light a mechanical match, even, maybe, with disdain. All the names are all the names. Like Vito. Vito lives there, no there, he lives there, yes, that's right where he lives. When he wrote leaving he decided to writing for a living. I eat sparsely, like a bird. I could tell you the story of blossoms in the dust with greer garson & walter pidgeon, I could tell you the story of giant, with elizabeth taylor & james dean & rock hudson, I could tell you the story of the world the flesh & the devil with harry belafonte & inger stevens & mel ferrer, I could tell you the story of night must fall with rosalind russell & robert montgomery, but at this late date. And So David & I got lost in middle village & I said we should go to Neiderstein's but when we got to metropolitan avenue we didnt know which way we should turn, and just as we turned, we saw Neidersteins, where I was supposed to have my wedding reception. Now what happened was I slept with my fiance's best friend & then I called off the wedding, dress & all & the next day Neiderstein's burned down, wooden fans & all. But the wooden fans were still there & David had two vodka gibsons which means they have pickled onions in them, which he made me eat one each of, and I had two heineken's in frozen glasses & what did we watch but a wedding & talked about queers that we knew & people in show business. Now David's frozen glasses were different from mine, you have to understand. And the wedding people were also frozen & we were frozen in time, like black holes, and so on. On the ergosphere, if you know what I mean, the even horizon of a collapsed star. No we didnt talk about structuralism this time. So I left for the second time. And David predicted in the middle of mid-vil in Neidersteins that the man across the bar was a politician & that he would kiss the baby. So the man kissed the baby & all life was subsequently renewed, except that I had been staring. But we did not, something I cant say here, but that is another story, something about women. Now this room seems ominous, since I planned the crime. All the e's and o's of the entries are clouded, the a's too & the people outside are screaming, not planning for the world's restoration. All the names are all the names. They match, at least once, at least one time. Such will as that. We pass right by it unattended. Let me make them up—Anthony, Carmine, Mona Lisa, skip it. Those are childs, and childs room for us, with crayons in it. He wouldnt give me any of his money—strong, a sane one, a Survivor. Ceasing to make sense, listening, with money maybe with jokes. After the funeral of the rabbi's wife, all the people returned to his house & found him fucking the maid. "What are you doing," they asked. "In my grief do I know what I'm doing?" he replied. Ceasing to losing track, something about section 5, no. B-40, no 74. You are addressing you to me. I am addressing you to you. Too seldom a point of opening. Private space, opening private, opening space. I cant deal with the lost or last section. Not aside either. The joke: do you know people are dying to get in there; the joke: Vito lives there, no there, no here, at least wherever he lives or something, pointed out. Vital, vital force, vitalism, vitalistic, vitality, vitalization, vitalize, vitallium, vital principle, vital statistics, vitamin, A, B, C, D, E, G, H, K, P, &, X & different kinds of B were present, I wont go through their uses & statistics. There are 10 mg. of energy available in a dose, no more. More & your blood would thin like the blood of a rat who leaves the house & dies. What are these vitamins good for? Something about duty, I cant go into it now. Vitaminic, vitascope, in the childs room, in the nursery. This is my new, something I cant say, a female figure, say, 10 volts of her, matter least of, and her standing will. Whaddayou want? To let most be least past, but let most be most past, at least, standing still & seeing *you*. I'm starved. It could be, and that's past or that's this. A twister— you're lost. I lost one, or two or three or four more, lost four in a row, lost some in the rosebush, no film of this. Nothing & nothing a film. Snakes up here. Sneakers on. You cant hear me. Few have I parted with and still. Few have a single place like the place I lost. I am the scapist, the stalker, the shafter, I wear a scapular. I am the queer & the whore, at least sitting behind glass windows playing with stage prop glass balls, now, and not before, something I cant say here, at least I have nothing to do, at least it's ambitious. But she, she is different, she keeps the same phone number so as to always be accessible, like the you get wills, to those beyond, something I cant say here, in New York. All the somethings I cant say here, it's just New York. Some matter. Changing & moving. Likes weakness, I dont. So I do. So I do all the work, moving & changing like a twin of weakness lost. It's just New York, something I cant say here, if I hadnt stayed here. Sense of last chance.

Eve of Easter

Milton, who made his illiterate daughters
Read to him in five languages
Till they heard the news he would marry again
And said they would rather hear he was dead
Milton who turns even Paradise Lost
Into an autobiography, I have three
Babies tonight, all three are sleeping:
Rachel the great great great granddaughter
Of Herman Melville is asleep on the bed
Sophia and Marie are sleeping
Sophia namesake of the wives
Of Lewis Freedson the scholar and Nathaniel Hawthorne
Marie my mother's oldest name, these three girls
Resting in the dark, I made the lucent dark
I stole images from Milton to cure opacous gloom
To render the room an orb beneath this raucous
Moon of March, eclipsed only in daylight
Heavy breathing baby bodies
Daughters and descendants in the presence of
The great ones, Milton and Melville and Hawthorne,
      everyone is speaking
At once, I only looked at them all blended
Each half Semitic, of a race always at war
The rest of their inherited grace
From among Nordics, Germans and English,
      writers at peace
Rushing warring Jews into democracy when actually
Peace is at the window begging entrance
With the hordes in the midst of air
Too cold for this time of year,
Eve of Easter and the shocking resurrection idea
Some one baby stirs now, hungry for an egg

It's the Melville baby, going to make a fuss
The Melville one's sucking her fingers for solace
She makes a squealing noise
Hawthorne baby's still deeply asleep
The one like my mother's out like a light
The Melville one though the smallest wants the most
Because she doesn't really live here
Hawthorne will want to be nursed when she gets up
Melville sucked a bit and dozed back off
Now Hawthorne is moving around, she's the most hungry
Yet perhaps the most seduced by darkness in the room
I can hear Hawthorne, I know she's awake now
But will she stir, disturbing the placid sleep
Of Melville and insisting on waking us all
Meanwhile the rest of the people of Lenox
Drive up and down the street
Now Hawthorne wants to eat
They all see the light by which I write, Hawthorne sighs
The house is quiet, I hear Melville's toy
I've never changed the diaper of a boy
I think I'll go get Hawthorne and nurse her for the pleasure
Of cutting through darkness before her measured noise
Stimulates the boys, I'll cook a fish
Retain poise in the presence
Of heady descendants, stone-willed their fathers
Look at me and drink ink
I return a look to all the daughters and I wink
Eve of Easter, I've inherited this
Peaceful sleep of the children of men
Rachel, Sophia, Marie and again me
Bernadette, all heart I live, all head, all eye, all ear
I lost the prejudice of paradise
And wound up caring for the babies of these guys

Lookin Like Areas of Kansas

"We had our first cucumber
yesterday"
—Nathaniel Hawthorne

New England is awful
The winter's five months long
The sun may come out today but that doesnt mean anything
There are Yankees
Men & women who cant talk
They wear dark colors & trudge around, all in browns & greys,
    looking up at the sky & pretending to predict all the
    big storms
Or else they nod wisely
Yup, a northeaster
The sky turns yellow all the time
The river's grey
Everything's black or white
Everybody eats beans
Everthing freezes
Everybody lives in an old paper house
People chop wood all the time
They slide around on these slippery icy roads
All the trees look dead
They make long shadows on the snow
There's only daylight for about four hours
People sit home & drink boilermakers
At night all the telephones go out & the power lines blow down
Every weekend there's a storm so nobody can come to see you
The fireplaces are very drafty
The mountains look black
There are no books at the store
Religion's a big thing

Everybody has a history
Sex is drudgery for people in New England
It's 12° & they use Trojans or Tahitis
Some people have to have a generator
The windows are very small
You have to go out & get cold
All of a sudden the blue sky blows away
Everything's buried under five feet of snow
It doesn't go away until April or May
Everything's either apples or some kind of squash
The houses are all drafty boxes & you cant open the windows
People tell stories about each other
People have to come & plow the snow off to the side of
      your road
Then people shovel pathways to different cars
They have town meetings about the new sewer systems
The ideas of people in general are not raised higher than the
      roofs of their houses
Even the water freezes in the tap

Essay

I guess it's too late to live on the farm
I guess it's too late to move to a farm
I guess it's too late to start farming
I guess it's too late to begin farming
I guess we'll never have a farm
I guess we're too old to do farming
I guess we couldn't afford to buy a farm anyway
I guess we're not suited to being farmers
I guess we'll never have a farm now
I guess farming is not in the cards now
I guess Lewis wouldn't make a good farmer
I guess I can't expect we'll ever have a farm now
I guess I have to give up all my dreams of being a farmer
I guess I'll never be a farmer now
We couldn't get a farm anyway though Allen Ginsberg got one late in
     life
Maybe someday I'll have a big garden
I guess farming is really out
Feeding the pigs and the chickens, walking between miles of rows of
     crops
I guess farming is just too difficult
We'll never have a farm
Too much work and still to be poets
Who are the farmer poets
Was there ever a poet who had a self-sufficient farm
Flannery O'Connor raised peacocks
And Wendell Berry has a farm
Faulkner may have farmed a little
And Robert Frost had farmland
And someone told me Samuel Beckett farmed
Very few poets are real farmers

If William Carlos Williams could be a doctor and Charlie Vermont
    too,
Why not a poet who was also a farmer
Of course there was Brook Farm
And Virgil raised bees
Perhaps some poets of the past were overseers of farmers
I guess poets tend to live more momentarily
Than life on a farm would allow
You could never leave the farm to give a reading
Or go to a lecture by Emerson in Concord
I don't want to be a farmer but my mother was right
I should never have tried to rise out of the proletariat
Unless I can convince myself as Satan argues with Eve
That we are among a proletariat of poets of all the classes
Each ill-paid and surviving on nothing
Or on as little as one needs to survive
Steadfast as any farmer and fixed as the stars
Tenants of a vision we rent out endlessly

Carlton Fisk Is My Ideal

He wears a beautiful necklace
next to the beautiful skin of his neck
unlike the Worthington butcher
Bradford T. Fisk (butchers always
have a crush on me), who cannot even order veal
except in whole legs of it.
Oh the legs of a catcher!
Catchers squat in a posture
that is of course inward denying orgasm
but Carlton Fisk, I could
model a whole attitude to spring
on him. And he is a leaper!
Like Walt Frazier or, better,
like the only white leaper,
I forget his name, in the ABA's
All-Star game half-time slam-dunk contest
this year. I think about Carlton Fisk in his
modest home in New Hampshire
all the time, I love the sound of his name
denying orgasm. Carlton & I
look out the window at spring's first
northeaster. He carries a big hero
across the porch of his home to me.
(He has no year-round Xmas tree
like Clifford Ray who handles the ball
like a banana). We eat & watch the storm
batter the buds balking on the trees
& cover the green of the grass
that my sister thinks is new grass.
It's last year's grass still!
And still there is no spring training
as I write this, March 16, 1976,

the year of the blizzard that sealed our love
up in a great mound of orgasmic earth.
The pitcher's mound is the lightning mound.
Pudge will see fastballs in the wind,
his mescaline arm extends to the field.
He wears his necklace.
He catches the ball in his teeth!
Balls fall with a neat thunk
in the upholstery of the leather glove he puts on
to caress me, as told to, in the off-season.
All of a sudden he leaps from the couch,
a real ball has come thru the window
& is heading for the penguins on his sweater,
one of whom has lost his balloon
which is floating up into the sky!

The End of Human Reign
on Bashan Hill

They come down on their snowmobiles for the last time,
    come down to meet the car.
They're shouting, "Hoo Hey! The snow! Give them the snow!
    Let them eat snow! Hey! The snow!"
Looking like wild men & women, two wild children & a
    grandmother too, they're taking turns riding the
    snowmobile, they're getting out.
Hoo! Hey! The snow! freaking out.
Everybody in town watches, standing in groups by the
    "Road Closed" sign.
Shouting back, "Take it easy! The snow!"
On Bashan Hill they'd lived in a cloud, watched. They'd had
    plenty of split peas, corn, Irish soda bread, fruitcake,
    chocolate, pemmican. But the main thing was—NO PLOW!
Day before at the Corners Grocery, news got around. "They're
    coming down from Bashan Hill—never to return!"
The snow!
Hey, the snow, you forget. They're coming to get a beer.
Have another beer, smoke, jerk off & be thankful.
They're moving to a place above the store, where they can be
    watched. The snowman'll come & watch them, the pie
    man'll
    come & watch them, the UPS man'll come & watch them,
    the
    oil man, the gas man'll watch them, the plow man'll watch
    them, the workers on the town roads
Sink their shovels deep into the winter's accumulation right
    before their very eyes, eyes turned blue in the
    Arctic night.

The brown-eyed family from Bashan Hill in town for a
postage stamp.
The black-eyed family of deer, the open-eyed rabbits, the
circle-eyed raccoons, the white-eyed bear.
Where do the green frogs winter that look so old?
We watched so carefully our eyes became vacant, our minds
stirred from laughter all the memories of a chant.
Hoo! Hey! The snow!
They've come down the hill we watch in a cloud, night of the
full moon, icy crowd on the road watching them.
Have a piece of chocolate!
Open your eyes!

What Babies Really Do

Light like the life I'm in
Who said that did you say that did I
Eating doesnt go with prose
or poetry, spaghetti maybe

Out a window cool spring gray day
with only tips of trees in buds
The ground's not wet yet
Something leaps & bounds

Mothers always too specific
Ounces of pounds, silver on silver
I wouldnt actually eat a clam with a spoon
It's too rubbery

Often when I'm happy a fear comes over me—
not fear that the joy will end, but fear that circumstances
beyond my control and unexpected will arise to prevent me
from ever feeling joy again

We'll get dresses from Boston
like the elation of a sealed fruit
pure banana with the elation
of the afternoon in its skin

Rheingold kasha scotch kooler
I let endless thoughts go by in between
like the rice that looks like a belly
I dont have my own voice

So I quickly end the pleasure
of the first gray day that was truly
brown in the air, many trees
have snapped in half this winter

One big maple threatens the house
with its leaking bark, a crack
right down the side of an arm of it
We agree it'll fall but in what direction

Rice beads rutted road too many things
in my ideas, I like The New Yorker
where the poems have no ideas
I like the gray sappy maples losing their branches over me

The brown road's ok, smell of bananas
Birds are good, you live inside them
We found your slip you should see my view
You forgot to remind me not to have another beer

It's an endless afternoon, it refuses to rain
I fill up my mouth with Dashiell-Hammett-type smoke
It refuses to be consistent
As there are ingredients all over

& more branches, chair legs
& more flour, I sit with the food
Tuna tempter kasha varnishkas
A hundred and one fillets

Not just brown bread
but brown bread with raisins
You order more than five lbs of oranges
I carry a crate in the back of my jeep or keep

Sunflower kernels to replace the sight of one
Life like it is
The gray branches wont move
unless wind blows them

She's in motion as usual to the tune
It's a luxury to stay inside
I havent finished
singing outloud

Listen, gaggle gaggle
broo ah ha ha
thoughts unravel
run after her

The sun won the edge of the wind is cold two three
Nothing much but poetry
Ah ha I hear

Instability (Weather)

I would eat a lilac if it were a violet
Forcing the unstable air which is swirling around us
In the northeast to thunder & lightning
This air clears itself of clouds at night

We get the lilacs but have to abandon the rhubarb
To the new tenants, a few donkies & a goat
We get the first few mustard plants & some apple blossoms
We get the coldest air of the last frost, the birds
          arent even chirping properly

I must get back to the lilacs
So excited when I saw them first blooming in the back
          next to the apple tree
I nearly jumped for joy my heart beats rapidly
Because they are late & we are moving

Blossoms for Lewis & Charlotte who's here
The lilacs were so far away I didnt get to them
But I wont tell, I'll go with a scissor tomorrow
The scissor I'll hide in the woods tonight

For some strange reason I'll never say
I'll never have lived a more exciting day

Very Strong February

A man and a woman pretend to be white ice
Three men at the lavender door are closed in by the storm
With strong prejudice and money to buy the green pines
One weekend fisherman and blue painters watch
The vivid violet winds blow visibility from the mountain
Beyond the black valley. That means or then you know
You're in a big cloud of it, it's brilliant white mid-February
A week or two left on distracting black trees
Before the brownish buds obscure your view of the valley again.

Looking for company four dark men and a burnt sienna woman
Come in for three minutes, then bye-bye like a gold watch left on the
     chair
Or part of the sum of what big white families think up
To store for long yellow Sundays to eat for brown ecological
     company.
At some point later gorgeous red adventure stops, did you forget
To turn it down and laugh in the face of the fearful white storm
     anyway
Or picture it brilliant blue for a further Sunday memory
In a coloring book, you talk as lightly as you can
Refusing a big pink kiss, you burned the Sunday sauce
Of crushed red tomatoes, you turn it down to just an orange glow.
This particular storm, considering the pause and the greenish thaw
     before it
Reminds me in its mildness of imitating a sea-green memory that is
     actually
In the future, I imitate an imagined trumpet sound
Or the brilliant purple words of a man or woman I haven't met yet
Or perhaps it's a grey-haired man I already know who said some-
     thing yesterday

To a mutual friend who will give me the whole story in black and
    white tomorrow
Or the day after, just as the big orange plows for the local businesses
Go to work to push away the rest of the white snow that will fall
    tonight.

from *Midwinter Day, Part Four*

The Three Little Pigs. Three pigs who have hair on their chins are too poor to continue to live with their mother, they must support themselves. Two of them get eaten by the wolf because they build their houses out of flimsy materials. The third pig who has a brick house which he got by posing as a cripple, winds up boiling the wolf alive and eating him. Admiral Byrd was the first person to spend the winter alone at the South Pole. For a while he did well and wrote a lot of speculations on the nature of the universe, then the stove in his hut began to poison him with fumes. He would collapse all the time and he had to force himself to eat, he kept the heat on only enough to survive and as the winter got colder, ice began to cover the walls, ceiling and even the floor. He told his men nothing was wrong but his messages in code reached them as indecipherable gibberish half the time, so they made a trip in the dark to rescue him.

Marie's asleep. Sekhmet the wife of Ptah said, "When I slay men my heart rejoices." Depicted with the head of a lioness, she was so brutal and unrelenting that to save the human race from extermination Ra spread across the bloody battlefield seven thousand jugs of a magic potion made of beer and pomegranate juice. Sekhmet who was thirsty mistook it for human blood and became too drunk to continue slaughtering men. The human race was saved but to appease Sekhmet, Ra decreed that on the twelfth day of the first month of winter, there should be brewed in her honor as many jugs of the philter as there were priestesses of the sun. "Hostile hostile is the 12th," says the calendar of lucky and unlucky days, "avoid seeing a mouse on this day, for it is the day when Ra gave the order to Sekhmet."

Popped-out-of-the-Fire: A girl lived there (with her brother and grandfather). Though the girl slept alone every night some person came to sleep with her. The person who came to sleep with her never spoke. He came to her there a long time. And then the girl became pregnant. She did not say anything of it, she was afraid to. Now this is what she thought. "I will paint my hand. That is the way I will find out who it may be." Indeed that is what she did. And then (in the night) she hugged him, she put her hand on his back. Now the people (men) were going to come out of the sweat house where they were sleeping. And so she watched in secret, and then all those people (men) came out. Indeed now she learned it was her own older brother who was sleeping with her. Then the girl became sick (from shame and grief she no longer ate, and then she died), and he also died, he starved himself (in his shame and grief), and that is why he died too. When she died her father laid her upon the fire. And he held an Indian blanket and the old man spoke thus, "Pop out on to this here!" Sure enough the baby popped out (from her scorching corpse). Now its grandfather brought it up.

Septimius Felton was a character of Hawthorne's who tried to create the elixir of life from some old Indian recipes of his aunt's and the secret information given to him by a soldier he shot during the Revolutionary War. On the soldier's grave a red flower grew, it was supposed to have been the last ingredient, sanguinaria sanguinaris, bloodroot, growing from the heart of a young man violently killed. But the flower was a hoax planted by the Englishman's lover who seduced Septimius and helped him make the potion which was now a deadly poison, then she drank it, confessed all and died. Then Hawthorne intimates that Septimius who loved knowledge too much inherited the English soldier's estate and became a boring landowner whose descendants had dull and lifeless eyes.

Joshua the son of Nun sent men to Jericho to spy for him. They went to the house of a harlot named Rahab. She hid them from the king because she said she knew the Lord had given them the land and had dried up the water of the Red Sea for them. In exchange for her help they agreed to spare her and her family from annihilation if she would hang a scarlet thread from her window.

. . .

I steal from the bed not to waken Marie. She's happy to sleep but
will wake up angry. Sophia will wake up feeling good unless she's
cold. In the morning if the sun shines which now it hardly ever does,
Sophia gestures with grace towards the eastern window in her room.
I set fire to the end of a cigarette and look out the kitchen window at
the mess of ice on the trees, streets and roofs. No geese flying south,
it's the awful solstice. This morning the axis of the earth began what
the papers called its slow tilting return, the sun will last one minute
longer and the nights will be shorter. Lately when the sun sets it
breaks through the hat of cloud on the sky like a person on the street
who only glances at you, and then it begins to snow. The sun catches
your eye.

A calm sentence like a story. I used to know a man who had a
dog and I followed their steps in the snow, I got into the habit of
walking just as far as they did every day. At the same time I also knew
a woman whose husband had seven guns. I used to know a woman
who's the woman who married Neil Simon. I like the woman who
used to work in the Lenox market, she never wears boots, then she
retired. In New England the women are often more exciting than the
men, Lewis thinks so too, I don't know why. There's a tribe
somewhere where people say about the men, look how he's changed
since he's had children, he looks awful!

The soldiers came to relinquish and not fortify the wall and a
meal was made of fish from the brazen sea and wine in vessels of
brass and of every day that remained its work required that the day
be a woman and that the woman be pretending to be another
woman, that anger is the father and anger is the child, death is food
to remember history to tell, a big fat man with a white beard in a red
suit who eats what we eat and is never cold even though he flies
around the world in only air, dear mother, the church is still cold.

. . .

The language into which we put the order of stories from this kind of memory is a mesmerization of sins like the ones I made up which were my first stories because when I still had reason to confess I was free of even the venality of my tales, though told with love, and I could imagine coming up with enough lack of perfection to commit them or even obsessively put them in writing like a letter to a judge when I'm in prison, rather than just to speak them to one man who was a story in himself of a kind of outfit of supposed love which could turn to enmity or even lechery out of love, another love, in a minute, a story of the moment of the mystical body and cannibalistic frenzy laced with fierce and beautiful singing of songs in loud strong weak guilty and innocent voices below the organ tagging along behind the desire for a fantastic transforming love of what is beauty or ritual's idolatry of mystery among our historical family, all present in the church, though late, to tell us what to do next and how to have the pride to proceed.

Not the pride of devils who are fallen angels but the pride of angels who are faithful who subsume all love of other and the hideousness of possession under the vaulted ceiling which is standing for the life where the mind is like a sky over the earth and men and women are the homeostatic expressions of a universe given for a while to their multitudinous ideals of fateful love, land as homes and the principals of families and food, and the righteousness that activates the strongest of what's left of the men and women after wars are finished to excite the rest to some belief in gratuitous love and the inevitability of the sublime because life for almost everyone has its moments and but for that the whole thing is somewhat dead already, this was my great confusion.

The history of every historical thing including God but not including all men and women individually, is a violent mess like this ice. But for the spaces even hunchbacked history has allowed in between the famous and loud for something that's defined as what does please us. Which is perhaps this story of an intimate family, though you won't believe or will be unable to love it, driven to research love's limits in its present solitude as if each man or woman in the world was only one person with everything I've mentioned separate in him or she didn't represent any history at all though he or she had stories to tell and was just sitting kind of crazily before an open window in midwinter or thinking of the celebrating supper or sleeping on the independent bed or in the enclosed crib which in history could only be relentlessly plundered, in story a sensational death perhaps.

I am like a woman who says I am another woman, or a man who says I am another man. They sleep to rest, beginning to know another, like a story. Then we rest to recover something already gotten from what might be called its mother and father. Next our genius will amaze us like the rest we've had to discover of all we might ever be able to know. But not before, as the story now goes, the ones who discover it will be mythically lost having suffered wanting to unearth more than there is from what history's supposed to be, less than a baby, or the terrible criminal repeating memory which slows us down like a race a swift attack, a current of water in a river or the ocean's more famous undertow, this window of mine too badly designed to let air in yet too large to make sense, I only feel cold and I'm still here before it, young enough but still a mother, old enough to end the story that might have ended before me.

I have a sensation of waiting, you should call and tell me how the rest might go. Like an important letter, a whole different matter, if I only knew what I need to know. You call and I say in some way I already know all about it, I expected it. That's a story that might happen today. I don't dare to end as death is still bewildering, love might be a trick and you are another. But to be beginning I'll only say that to have you as love is like the history of this idiosyncrasy. If that is not a story then I who have so far listened so much and now am beginning to be able to say something, which is another story am surprised.

from *The Desires of Mothers to Please Others in Letters*

VISIONS OR DESOLATION

Come on, there's always the chance kids will do this, fight uncontrollably crazy screaming like howling buddhas and tearing each other's never cut before hair out, the bigger ones hitting the smaller ones on the heads with metal tops like latent homo- and heterosexuals with fierce exclamatory natures. Our plan is to just do everything ourselves without any babysitters for the next two weeks and then the classes are over, then we'll go to New York for a while again, the midwife said I had a neat uterus and she could feel whole arms and legs of the baby, I was waking and talking to a woman on the phone the other day about a playgroup and she kept using the word "shoot," kept saying, "Shoot I would do anything" and "Shoot I understand what you mean, yes shoot," then we'll come back here and spend January getting ready to have the baby, then the baby will be born at the end of that month, I can't find Dr. Spock can you? but before that we have to gather together all the things we need for the birth and for the baby, cotton balls and undershirts and roasted towels and a bureau for the baby's clothes and Marie needs a new coat, and we have to do some laundry sometime, when she plays outside now and squats to dig in the dirt the skin of her back is exposed to the air, and they both need new tights, there isn't any snow on the ground yet, it's easy to rely on the beat Poets when you're teaching, any more abstract stuff often turns the students off, they find Frank O'Hara much too difficult, I also want alot of red velvet material and a big red rug to induce feelings that can go past the moon, it's full again today, those regressive souls in my classes keep talking about how LSD makes deformed babies, these matches are called Rosebud because they have red tips of fire, so many times when you're pregnant people can't help but tell you all the worst stories they ever heard, I miss the part of Main Street in Lenox right in front of the bank where the crosswalk led across to the entrance to the library and the buses and cars came circling around the obelisk, Henniker's equivalent of an obelisk is a kind of former fountain on a triangular island at the foot of which is always lying an old apple core and a discarded ribbon, when I look up I see a portrait of a man holding a glove, if Russell doesn't see us at all tomorrow perhaps he'll think we're not there, I have only twenty minutes left if I'm going to get any sleep, what can I give you, is writing this offering? Lying in bed is a turmoil, anything can enter in, early tomorrow a woman will come with some children, she will be able to explain things to me about this town, she teaches cross-country skiing, now why don't I do something like that instead of wondering only about babies, poetry, the city, the country and the wisdom I was trying to talk to you about, yet I must've sounded a little corrupt when I said that. I do wonder also about you and your way of slumping in a chair which confounds your other way of looking like a jogger in pajamas, I shouldn't mention pajamas or everyone will make fun of me, I'm sort of looking forward to this January of heavy snows and waiting, bitter cold and never parting again for a while. I don't like teaching, it distracts us, it's like everything else everybody says is healthy, skiing jogging and sitting up straight and being independent, eating seaweed and living in the country, the protean brain, or the other way around: Montherlant is nothing if not protean. A peninsula is a body of land almost completely surrounded by water. Some old people live on one can of soup a day. A little peach in the orchard grew, a little peach of emerald hue. . . . I was reading this novel about a man who burned his girlfriend's house down and then later was almost completely the cause of her father's death and they try to make a case for this rogue being rather an expression of the girl's own destructive instincts so the book winds up without a sense of humor (ENDLESS LOVE) and so am I, it's better to go back to NOTES FROM THE UNDERGROUND for that. More subtle like the weather's blatancy (does that mean wind?). But I'm sure you never asked me for my opinions, you asked me for something of beauty, like the idea of

69

the constructing of a house, something less than esoteric, something formal that also has a use, a wedding song or a description of some semi-precious stones. How am I supposed to fit in to this life where children eat so much expensive fruit and leave their trucks in the sand to be run over by the diaper man, will the fleshy influorescence of a collection of color photographs still look like a pineapple or pine cone or a small bomb that looks like one of those? You and I like having each other to ourselves, I compare the two hands of the two yous but I still can't tell if the hurt one is swollen, why do we have so many injuries lately, is it wrong to walk into a door or let windows slam on your hands, to be slightly stabbed by the midwife to determine the iron content. . . . Something shifts and as Wittgenstein would say, and anybody else not normal, to take some pleasure in being obsessively careful, to quietly comb out the baby's hair and take one's time, to decorate the children with ribbons and whisper to them, to prepare special foods, secret inducements, to linger conversing about the dreams in bed, to encourage the counting of peanuts, these are the methods of the usual, inducements to the ordinary, to pass the time, to adduce pleasure, to encounter danger, to see silver spots before the eyes without fear, the safest form within which to take risks, the advertisement of the day's misery if I can still look up and see the man with the glove and a chance image of the accumulation of objects, the storehouse of pictures which will not work out in memory, there's only one time when you can't be doing this or that kind of work and have something like a drink make it easier than it is, and that's when you're giving birth to a baby but there's nothing new about that. I wish I could try it as a man for once and be the one watching nervously instead of the inhabitant of this always female body, always momentarily fertile and prone to that if I can use that word, it's worse than taking LSD, not over till it's over, hoping the baby will be born before another child wakes up, warning people that your screams are not real screams like in a movie or book, expressions of the forward movement of time or movements of the forward expression of time like words, in that case scream is to lean forward and make the time pass faster, hours by clocks in what they still call labor, different from plain work, working in contractions of the muscles of the . . . and so on, you know all about it I'm sure, lucidly there's space in between during which you feel like yourself again and that is like the book, then when the baby is finally born you don't know for a moment if you're thinking of yourself or the other, there's no reason why the words other and mother ought like an otter to rhyme, they didn't in Middle English, but then you wouldn't want to know the derivations for mother, the lees or dregs, I won't go into that, which is why it's difficult to remember to immediately hold the baby, you don't know the baby is different from you, especially if someone else is there. I had a baby once drawn out by forceps from my unwitting unconscious body and when I woke up I said, what was it. It's worth the tedious trip of consciousness with all the unnecessary pains to thus conquer nature with memory's astuteness, it's like the perception of color in after images. There is an end to the sensation, so of this letter.

from *Utopia*

I was working at my desk one night—Lewis had gone to Baltimore to give a reading with Lucille Clifton—& I was wishing somebody would come to visit me. The bell rang. The buzzer wasnt working and I couldnt leave the apartment because of the children. I hoped whoever it was, assuming it was a friend, would find a way to get in. One second later Grace was at the door, I dont remember opening it.

Grace looked even more unusual than ever, it was not just the patina of her bright red-bronze-copper hair & her shocking sensuality that blew my mind this time but a weird & intense sense of purpose which for a moment made me frightened she'd come to tell me some kind of awful news. Yet she was grinning at me. I couldnt understand how she'd got up the stairs so fast & I thought for a moment maybe it was somebody else who'd rung the bell and that I'd now have two visitors which often happens when you at last have one.

We kissed, Grace gave me a funny look & said, "I've just come from the future oh god Bernadette," & then she sat down. Luckily I had a bottle of Amontillado & had been drinking it mixed with some peculiar red tea this night. I brought her a glass and poured her a drink; Grace breathed deeply, drank and said nothing.

"What's going on Grace?" I asked, by this time obsessed with her state of mind, "What happened?"

"Bernadette," she said, "I've been in some other world."

"Grace calm down," I said though she didnt seem the least bit nervous, it was me who was having hard heart palpitations, "What world?"

"Well I cant begin this story at the beginning," she laughed, "and I cant speak generally either."

"Come on Grace you're driving me nuts."

"Dont say anything for a while," she said, "and I'll tell you everything." (She looked like she wasnt really sitting in her chair!) She said, "Last week I met two people in the country & they took me on a trip in their car. As it turned out we went about 25 years away, maybe more, I'm not kidding."

"Oh," I said, "are you o.k.?"

"Dont dont say anything," she said, "till I get started. But first let me breathe I am so relieved to have gotten here & to get to tell all of this."

"Ok," I said, "I'm not saying anything look and see." (It was very noisy.)

"The other night there was a knock at my door, it was just like the time the raccoon was banging at your door in Massachusetts, hanging upside down. I was a little scared at being alone, I answered & these two people were asking directions, or at least they seemed to be, then somehow in the midst of our talking it was obvious they knew me, they began without my telling my name at all to call me Grace & before I knew it & without it seeming spooky at all they were making all these big generous sorts of old jokes about me & my family & you & Peggy. That night I never thought anything about their knowing everything. Oh wait I've gotta describe them."

Grace breathed some more & I could tell she was only thinking of the story. It was hard to say nothing so I tried smiling at her in exactly the way she was smiling at me. It wasnt complicated. I took a further drink of Amontillado straight & felt a great rush of anticipation & love.

"They looked alot like Shelley actually, they were small and androgynous with her kind of big eyes & I couldnt tell, though it never occurred to me then to try, if they were women or men and women or what. They were wearing old-fashioned loden coats &

pants & one had on a bright Persian blue shirt & the other had a New York Aquarium shirt with whales on it. After we talked for a while they offered to show me their technique of flying. They hovered about the ceilings then, singing a light-hearted song about sleep:

'Sleep sleep sleep
I do I do I do
we're all balls of ears
two by two
it's me hot sun
blue sky at night
all knit together
darkness is light
half of one
becomes my twin
one hand is thick
the other is thin
transparent sky
lets me go through
in sleep each night
each of you
one of us is
brilliant weather
little sleep
statue mother
little sleep
statue father
someone anyone
and another'

"I know I slept then though I cant remember how I got to sleep & you'll laugh when I tell you I had a great dream about sex in which it was raining milk because of the snow in a movie & next morning when I saw the sun I knew I remembered something that should fill me with either pleasure or fear but I felt like I do in dreams all the time & I couldnt be scared or notice any other sensations in my body, I just felt even like a body with a mind moving.

"We left on our trip together without talking about it after we ate a big breakfast of Irish oatmeal with cream & tea. We went in their car which was a kind of Peugeot, modified to have 3 rows of seats & the whole inside was painted red. For a long time it seemed like we were travelling over the hills themselves, you didn't notice the roads. We talked about politics, sex, money, books, and music and dance, till, around noon, we arrived at a kind of camp. My friends introduced me to some of their friends and together they cooked for all of us a meal of pumpkin soup and grilled cheese sandwiches. Then we took a big pail of some peculiar dark beer down to the pond & sat on the shore to have a conversation. They had something interesting to smoke which made you feel like you'd been in a steam bath. We were watching the sun set & as we watched all these people began describing it to me in such a new and fanciful kind of language with all kinds of new words for everything that seemed more like the truth or accurate that at some point if they told me the sky was purple I could see a purple sky & a yellow mountain, but then it was obvious that was exactly what I saw and besides all that that wasnt what they said, it was something even newer, I cant remember, wasnt it just a simple sunset?"

Grace paused. "I dont know," I said.

"It was after that they took me into the future on such a long and thorough trip I cant begin yet to tell you all the details of it, but wait and let me tell you all the rest first. We all ate another meal later, again I cant remember, it seemed like mashed potatoes with garlic and maybe cream or something combined like that, then we made love & I found out that these people were female & male indeed in a way, there were all kinds of funny aerial acrobatics where two of them hovering were enough to hold me up & as long as one person was paying enough attention to another person you wouldnt fall down, but when you did they sang a funny song as you hit the ground & got kind of scooped up again with all the more attention & love & the song said something like: 'Small world (laughing) whole world

75

all set up, I see alot of (laughing) in your ah your mama & your papa,
let's laugh through your (penis) we will get to be laughing inside your
(vagina) because you see my sweet mouth has words in it, all the
sounds. . . .' I cant sing the song exactly but that's what it was.
They were teaching me too all kinds of lovely & intricate tricks."

Grace looked at me long enough so I couldnt help but say,
"What kind of tricks?"

"Well wait, wait, I'm wanting to tell you how I got here, and
then I'll be finished in a way with some part of the story & can
answer everything about the rest, because by then I'll be sure not to
forget everything. I must've slept again and in the morning, which
was this morning, we made a plan to meet again next week. They
said the revisions of life I'd remember might seem inconsequent
because they were just in our world but after more time I would even
remember more. I'm supposed to bring you and Peggy with me next
week. Then they took me here, to your door, in an instant, though
now it's night, and I dont even remember coming up in the elevator.
And now my story's done."

Grace seemed flabbergasted but she couldnt have been more
amazed than I was. All her exhortations not to speak which were so
hard to keep to before, seemed to have their effect on me now. I
couldnt say a single word. If I'd thought Grace were even sitting on
her chair, I might've thought at that point she would just fall off of it,
but since neither of us seemed to be subject to any of the effects of
gravity or any normal thing at all that we knew, we both seemed to
float staring at each other for an unaccountable while and then
we burst out laughing. Just before that I had had the thought "but the
elevator's broken" and then we laughed so hard and so long we
thought we would die laughing and lose our minds and by the time
we could conceive of stopping laughing we were moaning from so
much laughing, we began throwings things about the house in such a
way, if anybody'd seen us, they'd have thought we were lunatics.
Finally I grabbed Grace's arm & shouted as loud as I could, "What
did you find out!"

Concluding Unscientific Postscript

The pluralistic yellows of fall's sun
Scare the wits out of me and my daughters
In between the artful leaf shadows
You dont wanna mention slow reactions
To the merest daily sounds

You can feel a new device in your mouth
With wonder liquid bread with healthy head
If clean the art that's wrought by pen or type
Day after day why not relent to love scared
In silly cleanliness new artifact hence

By all that's kind I beg a natural helper
As a valuable book falls sophistically to floor
Of the joint we share without equal metaphor
Till August heedlessly makes something end
I wish my friend you'd love me against

The wishes of everyone sensible
I am certainly not so beautiful as to presume
Like the meanings heard on streets & avenues
& trials on country roads I learned about you from
That I would be more well from your acquaintance

Like the fooling afterthought of a notorious well-wisher
The glass might know what its warmer heart did not
& if I meet with men who dont believe in even speaking
Phosphoric, I'll expect a relentless well-nourished neglect
Like the natural equation of lovely lakes to swamps

& red the rug it falls criss cross without
Seeing heraldic my dumb ass so-called suffering
Cause I look ok but I cant continue on
So let me fall by form of spurious need of end
Near your cock & cunt, transforming friend.

Watching the Complex
Train-Track Changes

To Men

You put on an ornate ballgown
You say "someone has to do it"
You take me to where you work,
The inside of a pyramid with chasms,
Watching the complex train-track changes
Products and objects make love to my father
Two babies are born—Bruno and Daisy
You take your shirt off looking boylike & lovely
You get on the plane, both clown & wizard
And then get off in a comedy of manners
Our dates become a comedy of dinners
Your name rhymes with clothes
Your plane folds & flies away
Without us, I'll make the next one
We are enclosed in spaceless epics by breathless bricks
& still we'll meet like runes or the leashes for hawks
Let's go! Can we stay? Go to sleep.
A tree wouldn't talk or weep if I-forget-what
And you in the train's opulent rooms
Switch your cock to a baby and then say
"Must there (not) be a law against this?"
You add, "I have been thinking of you in my head"
You wear green glitter on your shirt instead of
A tie, that's how I recognize you as you
You are the prep cook the sous-chef you make
Duplicating potato salad like the loaves & fishes
You create gorgeous paper-like sculptures of foods
We go down in the car through threatening snows

To arrive in a second to eat in a renovated place
You and I tell "what" we are at the end of a movie
Our podium of soft loud feet flies by accident
I take the train to your house to hear Shakespeare & Verdi
Everyone applauds when you walk in. The director
Holds up each actor & describes his physical being
I talk to your father but only by telephone
You have the royal blue 8½ x 11 notebook with the lock on it
I want one but you say you cant get them anymore
I walk twice through that city I've been in before
All through its rooms, its streets and its Commons

A Woman I Mix Men Up . . .

A woman I mix men up
In my dreams & other ways, I wonder
If this is the same as knowing
What is & is not socialism, a man I'm sure

Does the same thing, mixing up
The mother for the lover or
Vice versa not to mention the mighty
Homosexual mix-ups which happen
Just as much, oh god whoever

He or she might be, I ask you
Why is David Lewis or Lewis Ed?
Why Anne Catherine or Catherine Ted?
Because I am not or dont want to be sure
I raise these questions to the heavens
Wherein I might, as proposed by a child
Sit on a cloud risking falling through
Should the child know a cloud is not solid
& should she bring no parachute, I feel

The risk's as great in loving as it is
In voting & your my lover's meeting even in
Dreams this other woman or man of your own sex
Seems like the newspapers, all too predictable
What types in what outfits'll appear
Doing what in what postures, suits & poses, to remake

The world is something not enough people dream of, one
Shouldnt use the word dream & one shouldnt use
The words should and shouldnt, cast off the book & find
No expectations, understanding liberalism's not
The same as conservatism or (god forbid) mysticism, there is
Morning and there is midday and there is night, there are
Phases of this one moon factually attached to the earth

Scatter the dictionaries, they dont
Tell the truth yet, I mix up words with truth
And abstraction with presence, who cares
Without a form who I am, I know I will timely die
But you two, God and this his image the junky bomb
Live forever to destroy the eternal the immortal
In what they used to call Man, now not.

Eight Blocks

for Bill Kushner

A very nice little purple dress
A box of colored film cans
A man with flowers for his Other, then another,
European women walking arm in arm
How lonely I am in this long line
Cops saying it's not sensible to be
Pretty women of ethics, she sighs, I gesture,
She says, if you walk fast you get tired and if
You walk slow you still do, she forgot I forgot
The elevated fingers of the sun we sang
In just voices to virgin Mrs. Kerchief-Cane
(To backtrack on a walk's ok) who was that man
Who knew what was behind me, now it's gonna rain,
Wind on the fat man's flat sequins
There are two different sides of the street
Between them is the traffic of the avenue
There are four corners on which to meet,
French cigarettes in the Arabian window
Then safe in the sweaty public school
But mothers and fathers are too early
To rescue each baby from a day of rigidity
Parents mass as at disasters and hide on steps
They peek in the window of the locked room's door
There's that woman I saw this morning
Carrying her cigarettes like a wedding bouquet

The Garden

for Adam Purple

Close to a house on a piece of ground
For the growing of vegetables, flowers & fruits
On fertile well-developed land
Is a delightful place or state, a paradise
Often a place for public enjoyment
Where grows the alyssum to cure our rage

Oriental night of the careless developers
Carpet of snow of the drugged landlords
Basket of gold the city's confused
Royal carpet of its bureaucracies,
Bored with bombs
Political ones of the complicated governments
Now stick up the very orb
For its nonmetal yet golden remains

Competing with the larval corn borers
The salaried test-borers
Imminently lead anti-sexually down to the foundation
Of the annihilation
Of a circular garden in which live members of
The mustard family
The tomato or nightshade family
The poppy family
The geranium family
The aster family
The mint family
The thistle or aster family
The violet family (heartsease)
The lily family

The cucumber or gourd family
The rose family
The composite or daisy family
The parsley or carrot family
And other families
(I dont think the pokeweed family lives there,
It earns too little or too much money per year)

We are told to swallow not a rainbow
But like the celandine the juicy proposal
That the lemon balm of low income housing,
Applied like ageratum to the old Lower East Side
(As early matured as the apricot)
And probably turned by deeply divided leaves
Like a rape of grapes before it's all over
Into the poison tomato leaf of middle income housing,
Cannot coexist with the gleaming black raspberries
In an ancient abandoned place
Around Eldridge, Foresight and Stanton Streets

We're asked not to think, like pansies do
That the pinnately compound, ovate, lanceolate, non-linear,
        lobed, compound, toothed, alternate, opposite,
        palmate, heart-shaped, stalkless, clasping,
        perfoliate, and basal rosette-ish leaves
Can heal like the comfrey
And cause to grow together
The rough hairy leaves of the city's people and
        the rough hairy leaves of the sublimity of
        a gardener's art
Made with vegetarian shit & free as cupid's darts

If all our eyes had the clarity of apples
In a world as altered
As if by the wood betony
And all kinds of basil were the only rulers of the land

It would be good to be together
Both under and above the ground
To be sane as the madwort,
Ripe as corn, safe as sage,
Various as dusty miller and hens & chickens,
In politics as kindly fierce and dragonlike as tarragon,
Revolutionary as the lily.

Sonnet

Love is a babe as you know and when you
Put your startling hand on my cunt or arm or head
Or better both your hands to hold in them my own
I'm awed and we laugh with questions, artless
Of me to speak so ungenerally of thee & thy name
I have no situation and love is the same, you live at home
Come be here my baby and I'll take you elsewhere where
You ain't already been, my richer friend, and there
At the bottom of my sale or theft of myself will you
Bring specific flowers I will not know the names of
As you already have and already will and already do
As you already are with your succinctest cock
All torn and sore like a female masochist that the rhyme
Of the jewel you pay attention to becomes your baby born

Sonnet

It would be nice to lose one's mind my mind
I'd like to lose it I wouldn't mind at all
To be in the lunatic asylum at last
All for you and for the taxi drivers

I'll go and be asked what year what day it is
& who's the president, how come he's a resident
I could teach prosody there but nobody
Knows what it is
So send me away to anybody
Anywhere who might
Not know something I might not
Since I must vice versa live

Whaddya mean perforce?
Army or navy or marines?

Warren Phinney

A little boy on August first night
Got into the colors possible in the light
Of this universe & of his cock
We spoke the words the little boy
My little boy like in the liturgy & in the litany,
Thee, more august that is magnificent
Than any of the daily concerns, his soft skin.
And losing my judgment I forgot about his Volkswagen
Which was needed in the morning to carry his father
And his mother to work, it was not his car
But the drive wasnt far and before you left
After the phone calls we answered
From friends to find you there was time
For another mention of the Russian Revolution
Then I wound up with my feet at the head of the bed
Knowing hippily about our stars, your guitar
& the meeting from which we fled, the proper porcupines
Having eaten enough of your parents' car's gaslines
To give us time to make the little more love
We'd dreamed of before the tow truck came.

Holding the Thought of Love

for Bill DeNoyelles

And to render harmless a bomb or the like
Of such a pouring in different directions of love
Love scattered not concentrated love talked about,
So let's not talk of love the diffuseness of which
Round our heads (that oriole's song) like on the platforms
Of the subways and at their stations is today defused
As if by the scattering of light rays in a photograph
Of the softened reflection of a truck in a bakery window

You know I both understand what we found out and I don't
Hiking alone is too complex like a slap in the face
Of any joyous appointment even for the making of money

Abandoned to too large a crack in the unideal sphere
        of lack of summer
When it's winter, of wisdom in the astronomical arts,
        we as A & B
Separated then conjoin to see the sights of Avenue C

Sonnet

I am supposed to think of my personal dot
I do and it is dull if you won't call
Who cares Angel I could find you even within my wrist
Nobody minds because of sleeping, I detest it myself
Why doesnt anybody want to demand to make love
Female to actual famous female or vice versa
Warm indoors is the repeating of the trivial of something
It doesnt matter what, I'm tired of not

Absence like parents is the astrophysical
What who knows come in I've got my birth control out
Come by get lost the curtain if fictionally red is not then real
Nor's the blood shed why for what, we warn televisions of it
Dont say anything bad like fuck or shit or otherwise & besides
You might have to wear ostensible clothing & hairdos all your lives

A Chinese Breakfast

Is it so far to the door?
Does Max's sandwich diminish my confidence to reach it?
Do fears as unnatural as dreams to waking
Reflect something of anything for everyone else?
Should madness ensue, would the tiny hole
For a dislodged nail in the wall be its focus?
Does the belong world in you?
Did the finch devour the bluejay
Right in the cleft of the dead bird of paradise?
Did a she slip the awful cup?
As spring comes a man's apple juice emits an ankle bracelet
And you're as forlorn as the mean dentist's smock of our culture
Plus a he can't find a parking space cause the ice is still thick
As the thief of the way a day might memory look

Sonnet

You jerk you didn't call me up
I haven't seen you in so long
You probably have a fucking tan
& besides that instead of making love tonight
You're drinking your parents to the airport
I'm through with you bourgeois boys
All you ever do is go back to ancestral comforts
Only money can get—even Catullus was rich but

Nowadays you guys settle for a couch
By a soporific color cable t.v. set
Instead of any arc of love, no wonder
The G.I. Joe team blows it every other time

Wake up! It's the middle of the night
You can either make love or die at the hands of
                    the Cobra Commander

———————

To make love, turn to page 121.
To die, turn to page 172.

93

Sonnet

Other than what's gone on and stupid art
I've no even memory of people and their part
In bed I forget all details
The female with the male entails
For whatever that's worth who cares
He who worries or she who dares
To die practically without mentioning
Again our idiotic utopian friendships

All the city's a mass of slush and ices
You might know I dont about poetries
My hand's your hand within this rhyme
You look at me this is all fucked up time
I'm just a sparrow done up to be
An Amazon or something and he? or thee?

We Eat Out Together

My heart is a fancy place
Where giant reddish-purple cauliflowers
& white ones in French & English are outside
Waiting to welcome you to a boat
Over the low black river for a big dinner
There's alot of choice among the foods
Even a tortured lamb served in pieces
En croute on a plate so hot as a rack
Of clouds blown over the cold filthy river
We are entitled to see anytime while we
Use the tablecovers to love each other
Publicly dishing out imitative luxuries
To show off poetry's extreme generosity
Then home in the heart of a big limousine

Homeopathic Busyness

Rigorously going from field to field
To plow up the internecine wars, how do
People find the time for their suppers
Or lost articles, there's so much blood
On the precinct steps even in the imagist snow
And I go from the moments are becoming tinier
To soon it will be bloody tomorrow's being over
Instead of any extent of thought's, love's
Or work's privileges big enough to be
The right doses. I make little money at it
But then who doesn't wake up at 6 am to think
Before the grapefruits' eyes, the student cereals
Floating around in, of all things, some milk
Before the window's corridor where the snow flies up

Incidents Report Sonnet

for Grace

Woke up from dream on
July 9 1965, dream was erotic
(can't remember what was in it),
I think the woman was attempting
to sit on her chair while
lifting the man's wallet
but then on the boatride my hand
got caught in the elevator door
by the firecracker tossed in
by a child who was a woman as missing
as the coffee money, anyway I
lost balance and, falling, woke up
jerking off through the chair,
another chair, was still falling
on my foot, sorry.

Incidents Report Sonnet #2

for Grace too

I was not yet married when
at age 2, a female other, I
put my finger into the forms of address
of the most blue night early in the morning
and said to my sister Rosemary, "Well,
what do you think of this!"

At the time we were both
sitting on the floor before the balls
of blue glass we were to clean
so often in the future and by the window
Rosemary once fell out of, who agreed
our exploration was fascinating

Only trouble is
Our mother hit the ceiling

Incidents Report Sonnet #5

for Grace also

Now you must remember that bed
we slept in head to feet in upstate new york.

David who was probably four
had just so badly injured his foot.

We had scared the wits out of the kids
playing hide & seek outdoors in the dark.

We ate Canadian Oat Bread and baked
millions of potatoes for our charges.

You and I took notes on everything
including Colin's dream ravings.

I'm forgetting to mention many things
including attempting to swim in the shallow stream.

Then we got into our tiny bed together
with our shared immortal fear of love.

Sonnet

ash	Ash is left behind from things
laugh	As I love to see you laughing when you come
drink	Or even drink—boom, wow! a wild boy
plate	Bring those damn apricots on a gold plate
crack	Before bottles in the park go crack
walls	Toward wilder heroinistic walls and we
train	Must then get on the red & tan, not the train
traffic	Or that exacting traffic plane
pages	Between the pages of this your book
O.K.	Read by many O.K. people
know	Who know that stupid
noise	Noise is coming from the street
still	Still in the still night
independence	On independence day welcome death!

with Philip Good

Sonnet We Are Ordinary C'mere

Excerpts I love you from abstracts
So what who cares songs of one and
Experience of this is a case like
Whole and I am not from there I write
To you to say I know nothing as ever
No rhyming no everything there is
No proceeding no thinking you will be my
What will you be? And that is the end

Except for the instance
What are you wearing?
Why aren't you here?
Where'd you put the window?

C'mere
Tell me the rest of it

Sonnet

To perform for you, ask me why, shall I sleep?
You make love so beautifully I don't know what to do
You come and put your university hand
You've thrown yourself off the roof by now

A white dog chases a man around the park
Your school hand your rich hand your suburban hand
Cares if I come I am a woman & we women must both
Have babies & there's my mirror & there's my baby

I want one intent on your form like a room
Prepare food and eat it if the race would survive
The crystal lay like a comparison with wealth to you
I checked and you don't have your car keys

Can I believe her? So
Returned from the dead.

Sonnet

Beauty of songs your absence I should not show
How artfully I love you, can you love me?
Let's be precise let's abdicate decorum
You come around you often stay you hit home

Now you are knocking, you need a tylenol;
From all that comedy what will you tell?
At least you speak, I think I'd better not;
Often men and not women have to sleep

You've come and gone—to write the perfect poem
And not ten like men or blossoms, but I am profligate
I strike the ground for ruin while you sensibly sleep
And so in this at least a poem can have an end

How could you sleep, I go to wake you up
My Lysistrata, my unannounced rhyme

Incandescent War Poem Sonnet

Even before I saw the chambered nautilus
I wanted to sail not in the us navy
Tonight I'm waiting for you, your letter
At the same time his letter, the view of you
By him and then by me in the park, no rhymes
I saw you, this is in prose, no it's not
Sitting with the molluscs & anemones in an
Empty autumn enterprise baby you look pretty
With your long eventual hair, is love king?
What's this? A sonnet? Love's a babe we know that
I'm coming up, I'm coming, Shakespeare only stuck
To one subject but I'll mention nobody said
You have to get young Americans some ice cream
In the artificial light in which she woke

Clap Hands

I'll write you sonnets till you come
Home from school again, the music of your cave become
A stalagmitic presence, honey I don't have
An electronically regulated discharge tube that can emit
    extremely rapid, brief and brilliant flashes of
    light, such a squinting and twisting around
    as to disorder it's nice to divide a sonnet

This way when you might fuck me up the ass
On account of the presence of the bureau by the door
Cause of some song like the one by Tom Verlaine
Where he says adieu like a kid from Brooklyn

Tell like so cause me Bill loves you to not to know
Turn the hear to why over Bill me cause I'll know I you
Say and am to exist I not entranced pretty
Can't Bill with startling say Shakespeare myself that

Couplet I adore you it's my habit
I want manly things & should not, women come to me

Sonnet

For that which is not conscious, the
language provides no means of expression
—Gregory Bateson

You read about Uranus in the Times?
How there's two more moons? & how the guys
In the neighborhood I grew up in got arrested
For killing a final cop and wounding a woman one?

She's in stable condition, life is
Kind of hot if empty-seeming, don't you think?
Me and the cop who arrested him have got alot in common
Not only cause of Ridgewood and cause his name is Angel

My Voyager, Uranus is far away as far as my pessary
From the magnetosphere forgive me cock
Gaea was born of Chaos in a phoneless prison
Let's have a baby today, I gave

You a new name

The Phenomenon of Chaos

Love's not intent today what did I see
A bank, a store, a pattern of leaves
Fallen to the basketball court because
Rain followed the smoke of eleven states' fires

To exit from the universe you could
Believe nothing is checked on
But we don't exactly exist do we
Otherwise how could we

Do you love me when the earth's sun
Sets on your song on your tongue
This is ridiculous the universe
Is no longer uniform

By this we mean the universe's not or aint
A standard of nothing love's turning no more

Catullus #48

I'd kiss your eyes three hundred thousand times
If you would let me, Juventius, kiss them
All the time, your darling eyes, eyes of honey
And even if the formal field of kissing
Had more kisses than there's corn in August's fields
I still wouldn't have had enough of you

Catullus #99

Honey while you played I stole
a little kiss, Juventius, sweet sweet

This didn't go unpunished & from then I'm fixed
on the highest tearless crucifix
I make myself clear with my tears
it doesn't work and you're still mad

Once when we kissed you used your spit
to wipe your lips, oh your soft fingers
you looked like you thought you might get Aids
from the dirty kiss of this diseased whore

How come you always bring me love without rest
It's all misery, you always torture me
that small kiss was the bitterest

And all you've given me since are punishments
handed out like medicines for miserable love
I'll never steal another kiss

After Catullus and Horace

only the manners of centuries ago can teach me
how to address you my lover as who you are
O Sestius, how could you put up with my children
thinking all the while you were bearing me as in your mirror
it doesn't matter anymore if spring wreaks its fiery
or lamblike dawn on my new-found asceticism, some joke
I wouldn't sleep with you or any man if you paid me
and most of you poets don't have the cash anyway
so please rejoin your fraternal books forever
while you miss in your securest sleep Ms. Rosy-fingered dawn
who might've been induced to digitalize a part of you
were it not for your self-induced revenge of undoneness
it's good to live without a refrigerator! why bother
to chill the handiwork of Ceres and of Demeter?
and of the lonesome Sappho. let's have it warm for now.

Large Imitation Classical Lune

Patricia my man
you disapprove of men but
when we fucked
you didn't mind my boyishness
so very much
you said it reminded you
of my Sophia
now you and Beth attack
my new boyfriend
and say he hasn't anything
to say plus
he's just like other men
to idiot Bernadette
you say how I love
men takes time
from our conversations our privacy
but you don't
feel that way about Maureen!
Laura'd be horrified
to know which she does
that I speak
of you two as one
but, girlfriends, remember
the sky's the limit in
these risky questions
of friendship and of love
I've overcome all
my travel phobias, my fears
of enclosed spaces
I'll go to Staten Island
I'll go alone
Mommy and I aren't one

but I won't reform
I still wanna make love
to you two
as one and too, him

Hendecasyllables on Catullus #33

You have the balls to say you will be with me
but you hardly ever are, then you say you're scared
of your parents' opinion, they pay your rent
I wouldn't mind that if they didn't think I
was a whore ridden with Aids disease & worse things
but I am I and my little dog knows me
in the most astonishingly bourgeois way
I even pay my self-employment tax now
and put leftovers into expensive tinfoil
to be used in imaginable tomorrows
therefore I protest my bad reputation
but I do wander all night in my vision

Catullus #67

CATULLUS:

O sweet delightful delightful door, a pleasure to the husband
   and to the husband's father, bliss for all parents
   who have penises
Be in good health my door, hello to you, let Jupiter
   or God increase your self's good works
Door who serviced Balbus well and once upon a time
While he still held his own old seat in the home,
   that is, he lived
And to what extent, how much, do you bring bear carry
   back and backwards to swim to stream to flow to serve
   so badly
After the stretched out fact of the married man versus
   the dead man
In the old sleepy house to have been so abandoned . . .
Why have you become so changed to us?

DOOR:

So it please, Caecilius, son of Balbus,
whom I now serve, I haven't changed
nor is it my fault: it never was
No matter what anybody says
I've committed no sin
People will always blame the door
whenever a bad thing happens
Well, let them talk: I didn't

CATULLUS:

It's not enough for you to speak one word about that but
to do it so anyone can sense it and feel it and see it

DOOR:

How can I? Nobody wants to know the truth

114

CATULLUS:
Well that's what we wish for: you have to tell us
   things without a doubt

DOOR:
Well, first of all, she wasn't a virgin
when she came to us
It was old Balbus himself who had her first
because his poor son's limp dagger hung
like a withered beet that never even reached
mid-tunic; yes, it was the father got in the marriage bed
and defiled it
whether from pure lust
or simply the urge to do his son's work:
somebody had to do the proper thing
and undo a married virgin

CATULLUS:
He sure was one extremely high frequency father-in-law—
you speak too well of him—this parent pissed on the lap of
the wife of his son or maybe he pissed in her belly or maybe
he pissed on her breasts or maybe he pissed in a holy way
on his son's possession of his wife

DOOR:
Catullus, that's not all they say,
and not just in Verona,
but throughout all of Brixia,
amata mater meae,
along Chinea's watchtower
wherever the river Mella flows
everybody knows
she's done it with
Postumius and Cornelius

CATULLUS:
Now here someone will say, What? Door! How did you know
all about us without ever leaving the threshold? Without
hearing people talking in secret away from you? Aren't
you just fixed under a small beam to shut and close as
much as usual and to open and expose what's going on
in the domicile?

DOOR:
I don't have to walk
I can hear her talk in a low vioce
about all she does to her maids
She's not aware I have eyes and ears
I could mention one gentleman by name but I won't
though I can tell you he is tall
without lifting his red eyebrows
He was in court lately defending himself
but the pregnancy was false.

with Don Yorty

116

Two from the Greek Anthology

You mother
You're so fucking pregnant
But not feeling contrary
You turn over to have some fun
I'm rowing you
Over your great ocean
This labor's not small either—
I throw you overboard when
I come in your beautiful ass
I'm giving instructions
In how men love

—Dioscorides #54

You sing and play the lyre and I'm on fire
I want to strum the whole fucking universe
you know I want to loosen your strings

—Anonymous   #99

with Rosemary Mayer

117

The Incorporation of Sophia's Cereal

Two mad men and to mad men what poetry is
Fine lines written dumbfounded and high
& equally always the syncretistic goings-on
because everyone is furnishing everything
With the body they already have to live in
Beyond even believing in living, there was
This morning's bowl of puffed wheat, the bananas
Were the teachers, the cereals were the kids
And I Sophia said was the giant and
My spoon was my spoon

Max Carries the One

Dont look at me, look at your own self
In the given weather it's raining harder
The world is round & falling down, so rocks
Look out! it's nice to be exact as she & he
Fall like rain to a little bit lower than
Young & watching something without participating
Where you begin or above like snow flying up
The curve uncriticized by us, the child
The dumb drips exist when the sun
Beyond the stupid rectangles is the ancient flower
Shines on them? comes out? so what? criss-cross?

Counting nineteen humans plus eight trees equals
Twenty-seven living beings and that's all
And one is watching this something, you carry the one

Ode on

Everyone is dead handwritten
We keep writing anyway
There is a sought picture finish
Parentheses cross out hamlets
Arma virumque cano
I feint in imitation of a proven
You arch art act you do not
Belog to a particulate selx
We plan at the lakes & places
Let's hark to your ass daddy
So firm even without dactylls in it
Then meditate as dumb daughters
Laughing to be fooling with our
Female fellows, Father
If only you could see us

First turn to me. . . .

First turn to me after a shower,
you come inside me sideways as always

in the morning you ask me to be on top of you,
then we take a nap, we're late for school

you arrive at night inspired and drunk,
there is no reason for our clothes

we take a bath and lie down facing each other,
then later we turn over, finally you come

we face each other and talk about childhood
as soon as I touch your penis I wind up coming

you stop by in the morning to say hello
we sit on the bed indian fashion not touching

in the middle of the night you come home
from a nightclub, we don't get past the bureau

next day it's the table, and after that the chair
because I want so much to sit you down & suck your cock

you ask me to hold your wrists, but then when I
touch your neck with both my hands you come

it's early morning and you decide to very quietly
come on my knee because of the children

you've been away at school for centuries, your girlfriend
has left you, you come four times before morning

you tell me you masturbated in the hotel before you came by
I don't believe it, I serve the lentil soup naked

I massage your feet to seduce you, you are reluctant,
my feet wind up at your neck and ankles

you try not to come too quickly
also, you dont want to have a baby

I stand up from the bath, you say turn around
and kiss the backs of my legs and my ass

you suck my cunt for a thousand years, you are weary
at last I remember my father's anger and I come

you have no patience and come right away
I get revenge and won't let you sleep all night

we make out for so long we can't remember how
we wound up hitting our heads against the wall

I lie on my stomach, you put one hand under me
and one hand over me and that way can love me

you appear without notice and with flowers
I fall for it and we become missionaries

you say you can only fuck me up the ass when you are drunk
so we try it sober in a room at the farm

we lie together one night, exhausted couplets
and don't make love. does this mean we've had enough?

watching t.v. we wonder if each other wants to
interrupt the plot; later I beg you to read to me

like the Chinese we count 81 thrusts
then 9 more out loud till we both come

I come three times before you do
and then it seems you're mad and never will

it's only fair for a woman to come more
think of all the times they didn't care

I Am Told I Must Bomb
the Tappan Zee Bridge

There was a sumptuousness that could be shared like
sexual knowledge with children who've never made love,
once knowing everything it didnt matter that everything
was so known: I was 35 when she was born, so in 1945
she'd then be ten.
It's in the movies there is knowledge where is the time, he
said your family is my family, I like love, everything seen
repeat you're my family family brief closer to my
like love everything seen version of scary my lost,
I am told my lost family now it belongs to you to you
in the store we know nothing but that occasionally they
find like love everything bring snakes & lizards to you
no kidding to improve their differences, I like you
better storeowners than they who so giraffe you, I
am your multitudinous free family from nowhere, very
right waters

scifi lee ann

you are you are since you love to be
identifiable things you are the perilous
chance lover of the splashing blue finder (that is hell)
you dont wear a hologram or safety pin you are
I take them one by one both dude & dudette
you are the peristalsis of all our necklaces
you are the back & forth & to Mrs confused you
are backwards the ending is faulty you are funny
but it is impossible even the early spring moths leap around
you are the possibles I wait to leap to the floor to see
that you are ordinary but in the summer of love we get up again
you are evanescing great but with a language problem you
are a big earthquake survivors taken under martial law,
comma, revolution finally, you are in the bathroom again
you are written there is no wild & just as i say that
you are wild you are good and beginning I sit on you you
are ending in details that is the story no one knows
you are absent as the electronic Hitler you are scifi
you are yes but betrayed by robots you are roses you are
vague doctor's journals you are an alien or two or three
aliens you are the clothing and the blankets fall with mind control
you are we put them back, my precognitive computer game, you
are Arthur C. Clarke, you are the universal ranger you play
gravity soccer & cosmic ball I dont quite get the rest
you are I'll be gone soon you are a book a cure for cancer
you are cute and this is in order you are poets in the bathtub
you are levels of weird eternal life via something you are
picking up girls with awkward language plus you are boyfriend
you are dilemma but what one you are animals change things
you are back to school with good writing you are inside a
video or the computer game you are good at end what is your name?
you are no one will see a virtuoso there is no story
you are can you carry the baby elephant around you are living
under the ocean you are all at once the seventeen & the thirteen
who might or will convene with prepuce side of who knows what

Sonnet

Suck me my virgin
because we are welcome
as the casualties of the poor
move your cock sideways
& sit your cunt around
let's not go to the movie
it's too crowded for everybody
Tiddly Winks, World Map, Clash
Roger Rabbit, Mouse Trap
Solarquest, the Ice Cube game

Past hordes of girls & boys
Some of them are ours
Lesbians wake and go out to walk
All mothers together, the poison hydrangea

Marie You Must Meet Cristina at the Music School Tomorrow and Not at Her Home

for Fanny Howe

See the way the water chills the glass is not a story
written as fast as is said you should see the moon standing
out in front of the animals who just walked in onto the
ledges of the . . . no

They sit still as the squirrel paws to its mouth making
a sound of speaking after coming into the house, some of
the animals we see do not exist as

We drink warm water in the living room & a tracing is
made on our faces of the singing of the low & high notes
of all the failings of two dimensions like a chair that
lacks confidence to seat you at a concert of three kinds
of music summing up the work of the century with big bands
in the middle

Of the structure of water we are waiting in the wings in
& I push you into but you are too big or dead to fall
& you pick me up & carry me forward like some kinds of
sex and on my head

I am wearing my South African map-kerchief & the one
animal who chooses to move or attack is a wild snake whose
fangs we disconnect from the flesh of a person & then
the young women

Get together to put on the long right-handed glove that
carries a string for diving so when the descent from the
church's stainless steel disc set up as a decimated and
slanted pool platform is made, the string will still be
seen as the diver disappears

Into the part where you can finally see the non-sacred room
or school as a girl by the side of the underwater cameras.

It's good to swim in a church in a partial ellipse of its old
pool destroyed by what is built to interrupt its floors
& now we are gone just like many have houses to sleep in
with doors

I Want to Talk Now about Reason, Riddle

Meanwhile there is these reasons I keep thinking
that wheretofore nevertheless despite I'd like
to know about everything except death's dumb bite
without which we can all ride for quite a long while

I dont think it's tubular to write not no more
the only write I like is change the world ridden
so here's this riddle:

Gorbachev has a long one,
Bush has a very short one, the Pope doesnt need one
& Madonna doesnt have one at all???

Answer:
A last name.

Therefore there might be some importance in not writing forever
therefore to say never will I write till this world is changed
therefore to write till this world is changed without ceasing
therefore to write unceasing no matter what begin again

I Wish You Were Up Late, Gerard

His grandmother's dead right on the verge of
My loving him more than's allowable

Lucky I pour water over her body & worry
That hot's inexact or too late: my children's grades

Scattered all over the table despite the threat:
I didnt pay the last bill; they wouldnt send them

      Amidst the mail
More threats than ever, I want the cure now
I wont live without it, Max has never made love

To get to important love without what, please tell me

With the knowledge I now have, I dont want to write
Instead to make magic or to pay

Better magicians than I for the work without a serious
Alphabet A to Z 0 to 9 as the forethought of freedom
      Let me know

The Guild

On the exhaustive forest's farm
where wasted apples knock the fruit
from the staghorn sumac trees all night
she dreamed I might be dead
so she could have him in theory & then she
stole her sister's new girlfriend away.
He goes to bed early to sabotage our privacy
leaving me alone to talk and play with her.
(Also Antonio who wears loud flowered pink
& blue shorts & shirts says he likes her).
Late that night Joe & Linda's loud party
wakes him up but I wont talk to him at first
—maybe I should really be being mad at her.
Then he tells me he's jealous of how she loves me
And that's why he suddenly left the room.
This was the same day I got halfway down
a new path by the pond and turned back.
Now Nicky's just come home with two sixguns
from Wild West City which isn't far from here.

Death Is a Cambric Fabric

I've had my portion of prison
Ridden with person, desire's poison
Desire's person is an unruled idiot
I will wash the glasses now
The person's poison is a position
You dont have to cook to eat the food
Pay the rent it's not a portion of the person
Cant pay the portion of rent—you're a person in prison
Plenty of poisons in forms of potions
Available to all to allay
Deep emotions, that is, no agility to pay
The person who put you in the prison position
Of your city, your house in it
Your own poison landlord, poison govt
Poison company country prison on this poison earth
No portion of which is for each person
The fun is over it's getting dark
In the city & in the park
To crack the times
We are opposed in mind
Unwilling & disinclined
Too much sex entwines your hair
I dont know if the dawn is here dear
I want some grownup shoes
Like my female children have
I want the dawn to go back
To the darker femaler blue
It was just past sunset so that
Another isolated night can ensue, we never
Do anything bad, do we?
Hi ensuing logic
Please leave a message after

The sound of its intention
If you press the star button
When you get the machine
You dont ever have to listen to the message again

Sonnet

a little tiny poem
leaves us all alone

now that you're not here
dont ever come home

my cruelty only comes
from death's elaborate tombs

i talked to all your friends
talked to them one by one

they all agreed you are
a handsome child of nature

if so come here
as quickly as you can

if not I will unbraid
all the poems you said you made

The Ballad of Theodore

I saw my father
and then he was here
and dressed in a suit
he asked for a beer

I hadn't seen him
alive since 1957
dead I often see him
once in a while

He was all too calm
he was like a businessman
I got him a Moosehead
from the grocery next door

He'd walked into our school
daring and dead
"I havent talked to you in centuries"
"How good to see you," I said

He put on the head of a power animal
this time it was the tall giraffe
my father then wore a longer cloak
& I was shaking hands with his hoof,
            no kidding

It was quite a good time we had
he'd doffed the clothing of his absence
& no dead man is scared of being dead
& most of the living are full of this,
            his form of innocence

We conversed, it wasnt startling
I was twelve when he died
his new disguises were a method
to let particular animals as grownups confide

He foreswore the walls of the school
and that's where I lost him
no trick of time bemoaned his anxious fate
(I'm only fooling)

We drove cars backwards
ate acacia leaves, then
made witty conversation
wore bathing suits & swam together again

I lost him in the dream's sudden regular twist
like he was an aristocratic woman
going from supper to a game of whist
instead of what he really was—an electrician
                    who loved *Frankenstein*

I saw my father Theodore
& then he was there
a vegetarian ruminant silent giraffe
full of his new & current perfect past

All dressed in a suit as if quite dead
but only at first, then as mammal animal
he asked me for a beer, he said
"Here death is not emotional"

Sonnet

Swell is the attribute of leisure
Found dead in immaculate house
I walked by you I walked
right by you, she read me
The pretty good poem of my father
I can hear the pen click, the pen
Makes noise, I do have to finish my work
For money, let's count to six

And when at the beginning of a story
You I thank the blank rectangle of that blue
Fire escape experiment, it's a color
You can see because darker in minutes
Ending sky then never met did not
if not of something done, then imitation

Mums

The lord is pregnant & we are not likely
to make her not so to open the window
in her presence is the fragile pot of
potent tea, the white lilies that are really
called tulips, the upbeat miniature mums yellow
red as the poison poinsettia he whose
flowers are actually only leaves—they all sit
on the frozen table like a big thin flag trying
out inventing happiness thru complication of abstraction
as if democracy could not not outlaw things
or if a man what no no man could a woman did not
there was an appropriate absence of identification,
     this is no
secret message counted in ways time can afford
any average bunch of angels compare not to our lord

Failures in Infinitives

why am i doing this? Failure
to keep my work in order so as
to be able to find things
to paint the house
to earn enough money to live on
to reorganize the house so as
to be able to paint the house &
to be able to find things and
earn enough money so as
to be able to put books together
to publish works and books
to have time
to answer mail & phone calls
to wash the windows
to make the kitchen better to work in
to have the money to buy a simple radio
to listen to while working in the kitchen
to know enough to do grownups work in the world
to transcend my attitude
to an enforced poverty
to be able to expect my checks
to arrive on time in the mail
to not always expect that they will not
to forget my mother's attitudes on humility or
to continue
to assume them without suffering
to forget how my mother taunted my father
about money, my sister about i cant say it
failure to forget mother and father enough
to be older, to forget them
to forget my obsessive uncle
to remember them some other way

to remember their bigotry accurately
to cease to dream about lions which always is
to dream about them, I put my hand in the lion's mouth
to assuage its anger, this is not a failure
to notice that's how they were; failure
to repot the plants
to be neat
to create & maintain clear surfaces
to let a couch or a chair be a place for sitting down
and not a table
to let a table be a place for eating & not a desk
to listen to more popular music
to learn the lyrics
to not need money so as
to be able to write all the time
to not have to pay rent, con ed or telephone bills
to forget parents' and uncle's early deaths so as
to be free of expecting care; failure
to love objects
to find them valuable in any way; failure
to preserve objects
to buy them and
to now let them fall by the wayside; failure
to think of poems as objects
to think of the body as an object; failure
to believe; failure
to know nothing; failure
to know everything; failure
to remember how to spell failure; failure
to believe the dictionary & that there is anything
to teach; failure
to teach properly; failure
to believe in teaching
to just think that everybody knows everything
which is not my failure; I know everyone does; failure
to see not everyone believes this knowing and

to think we cannot last till the success of knowing
to wash all the dishes only takes ten minutes
to write a thousand poems in an hour
to do an epic, open the unwashed window
to let in you know who and
to spirit thoughts and poems away from concerns
to just let us know, we will
to paint your ceilings & walls for free

Say Goodbye to Legacy

you cant say
i think it's just
the best thing
he gets in
i ever liked
the gap

this is where
i woke up happy
they wanna go
walking down the street

that kind of language
i found
not reasonable
as if everybody
gets in
so many fights

dolls like this
great burgers
the cocoon
girl shopping

to everyone
my lost sense
your boyfriend
takes cares of
so many fights

they're not very
now say goodbye
I must've dreamed
I saw a dead guy

you learn from your girlfriend
your lost sense
has had so many girlfriends
their own money
cuddly to legacy
that i was happy
in a crowd of people

like take off your clothes
before you
their own money
so many fights
better than nothing
get into bed

Beginning Middle End

Rushed slowly up rushing stream road path
beginning at the interstitial meadow park
to see description we fell in past where
a recent tree had fallen bared wood color
of the mess of the pre-spring forest

Up & down root rock mud two-white-dot trail
right by Half-an-Abandoned-Smoked-Ham Corners
to the 2nd bridge where the postured guide escorted
9 times 9 some cynical hikers across, he shouted
"Space it!" We watched to wait to ask no destination

Cool air rushes to the hiking head by icier parts
Max straddles a downed tree to knock at dangling ice
Philip leaps to rescue my cooling blue bandanna from
small pools to small falls, strips a fine pine
walking stick, we hike back to watch methods
   of getting mud off shoes: roll em sideways in
   the dry dead grass; spray em with water like
   houseplants; change them for other shoes

Roll back to city through thousands of households
of cars to home of reminders & dumb attempts at order

Experimentation in Rubrics

I red will not be good
I red will not do what I should
I red will at random rubricate
Your beautiful ass tonight
You are my specific sentence
You're my first letter
My any A or letter else of any color
No one can hear our sounds
My words outloud are gone the sky's
Lost its unknown animals now it's
Black as the pen is law as are
So many centuries will pass before
You come home to my house I pray
You will conduct me glossily
In sex & its love proscribed
By all four of our parents
Tonight today now later
Like a title for a chapter
Of an illumined book

Manicatriarchic Sonnet

I am nothing but a list of things to do
this is not etcetera or red umbrella either
i think i did the things that might help others
for Marie for Danine for Wanda for the scifi writers
i started to write the letter about my new book of frowns
and then i stopped, mother, to see if you were around
only fooling you preventer of all my motion
i did though then want to see a big immobile tree
absent from the scifi histories of dignity
the way girls can talk without counting in
some fearsome sect of the absolute no one'd approve of
especially my bigoted parents who could love them

      talk girls talk on into the night
      there might be a second that rhymes with disaster

Marie Makes Fun of
Me at the Shore

for Bill Corbett

Marie says
look tiny red spiders
are walking
across the pools
& just as I am writing down
tiny red
spiders are
walking across the pools
She says Mom I can just see it
in your poem it'll say
tiny red spiders are walking
across the pools

Acknowledgments

Many thanks to the editors of the magazines and anthologies in which these poems and prose pieces have appeared: John Ashbery, Bill Berkson, Heather Booth, Cydney Chadwick, Laura Chester, Andrei Codrescu, Clark Coolidge, Michael Cuddihy, Bill DeNoyelles, Kenward Elmslie, Larry Fagin, Miven Findlay, Ed Foster, Peter Gizzi, Philip Good, Richard Grossinger, Bill Henderson, Jan Herman, Michael Lally, Gary Lenhart, Greg Masters, Connell McGrath, Tim Monaghan, Wendy Mulford, Charles North, Alice Notley, Ron Padgett, Michael Palmer, Todd Pinney, George Quasha, Tom Savage, Leslie Scalapino, Peter Schjeldahl, Michael Scholnick, James Schuyler, David Shapiro, Ron Silliman, Ethelyn Stearns, Chris Tysh, George Tysh, Anne Waldman, Barret Watten, and others.